The HIP-HOP
10

The Best of the Best that Shaped the Music and the Culture

CHRISTOPHER PIERZNIK

Copyright © 2012 Christopher Pierznik

All rights reserved.

ISBN:1477472436
ISBN-13: 978-1477472439

CONTENTS

	Intro	1
10	Labels	4
9	Underrated	14
8	Busts	20
7	Songs	26
6	Remixes	36
	Interlude	44
5	Beats	45
4	Albums	47
3	Producers	60
2	Groups	72
1	Artists	89
	Outro	114

CHRISTOPHER PIERZNIK

"Rap is something you do. Hip-hop is something you live"

- KRS-One

Intro

I've been a fan of hip-hop my entire life. Born in 1980, I'm just old enough to remember "Walk This Way," Run-DMC's video with Aerosmith, dominating the early days of MTV. Through my older brother, I learned about Eric B. & Rakim, EPMD, Boogie Down Productions and Public Enemy. In the process of introducing these artists to me, he created a monster. With each new artist and album, I wanted more. I was insatiable.

Throughout the 1990s, as I entered adolescence, my hunger only grew as the music also changed and matured. Snoop Doggy Dogg, Dr. Dre, Wu-Tang Clan, 2Pac, Nas, Jay-Z, The Notorious B.I.G., and A Tribe Called Quest all came to prominence in my junior high and high school years. It was a great time to be a hip-hop fan. But it was more than just the music. I wanted to learn everything. I studied the history of the culture, where it came from and where it was going. I've had a front-row seat as hip-hop has grown from being dismissed as a passing fad to becoming arguably the most popular musical genre in America. In the early days of MTV, the majority of hip-hop videos were relegated to one show, "Yo MTV Raps!," that was only shown late at night. Today, the network has an entire channel, MTV Jams, dedicated to those videos. Hip-hop artists routinely top the Billboard charts, sell millions of albums, sell out arenas, and win Grammys. It's clear that the music is not going anywhere.

There are four original elements of hip-hop: 1) DJing, 2) MCing, 3) Breaking, and 4) Graffiti. Everything else in the culture – such as slang, fashion, beatboxing, and even producing – grows out of one of these four elements. Since Kool Herc, the unofficial founder of hip-hop, first invented the break beat and others grabbed microphones and began putting words to the music, competition has been a ubiquitous component to the music. With its pervasive in-your-face bragging and hyperbole, hip-hop has often been compared to the sweet science and it's nearly impossible to *not* draw parallels between artists and boxers. (Throughout this book, the terms emcee, MC, rapper, and artist will be used interchangeably.) Much like a weigh-in in which two heavyweights pound their chests, the earliest lyrics revolved around emcees explaining how they were better than the other guy and everyone else within earshot. It's still true to this day. Whether in ciphers as showcased in the film *8 Mile* or on album singles in which successful artists flaunt their newfound wealth, it all comes down to competition.

The music has always focused on who is the best, whether on the microphone, behind the production equipment, on the turntables or, more recently, in the corner office. From an aspiring artist's first lyric all the way to an aging rapper's last album, the goal is to be the best. This book is an extension of that mentality. In the following pages is a collection of ten top ten lists, spread out over ten chapters, documenting the greatest of the great – artists, groups, producers, albums, beats, remixes, songs, labels, as well as the most underrated artists and even the biggest busts – in hip-hop history.

Of course, choosing the best (or worst) within a musical genre is strictly subjective. Even in sports, with the benefit of statistics and championships and winning percentages, it is nearly impossible to compare players between eras. In music, it becomes even more difficult. How does one define a 'classic?' How much weight should a person's influence carry? How important are record sales? What if an artist sells millions of copies of a debut album but never again reaches that level of success – does that make the artist a bust? Or is a bust in music similar to a bust in sports – the artist that seems to have all of the tools necessary to be a star but, for any number of reasons, never reached expectations?

Choosing the top ten of *anything* is only one person's opinion and the lists that you're about to read are my opinions, based on years of careful listening, in-depth research, and heated debates with other fans, writers, and industry employees whom I respect. I'm sure that they will have some interesting things to say when they read my choices.

I'm sure you will as well.

Without further ado, let's get to it…

CHRISTOPHER PIERZNIK

10. THE BEST HIP-HOP LABELS OF ALL TIME

10. No Limit Records

While it has been surpassed by Cash Money in recent years, Master P's **No Limit Records** dominated the genre for a short period and helped push southern hip-hop into the national spotlight in the mid-to-late '90s. Originally just a way for Master P to distribute his own music, No Limit rose to prominence with its patented formula of outlandish computer-generated album covers and LP's with more than 20 songs, most of which featured other members of the label (dubbed "No Limit Soldiers") that were almost exclusively produced by Beats By The Pound, No Limit's in-house production team at the time. At its height in 1998, the label released 23 albums, including Snoop Dogg's highly anticipated *Da Game Is To Be Sold, Not To Be Told*, Mystikal's *Ghetto Fabulous*, and Master P's own *MP Da Last Don*. Of the 23 LP's released that year, six sold at least a million copies (platinum) and four more sold at least 500,000 copies (gold). The success was short lived. Virtually every major artist fled the label over the next few years and No Limit eventually filed for bankruptcy in 2003. While it was reformed, rebranded as The *New* No Limit Records, and even found some success via the career of P's own son, Lil' Romeo, the hip-hop landscape had shifted and No Limit was left behind. In hindsight, it's hard not to laugh at the album covers or to watch the ridiculous video for "Make 'Em Say Uhh!," but No Limit introduced much of the country to the southern version of hip-hop and laid the foundation for a generation of artists (including Cash Money) that followed. There's a reason that Snoop, the first free agent emcee, chose No limit over every other label. For the briefest of moments, Master P's boutique label dominated the genre.

9. Duck Down Music

Originally created as a management company, **Duck Down Music** became an actual record label in 1995, based on the success of two of the management company's acts – Black Moon's 1993 debut, *Enta Da Stage* and the first album from Smif-N-Wessun (later renamed as Cocoa Brovaz), *Dah Shinin'*, released in 1995. Since then, Duck Down has been known as the famous New York hip-hop imprint that values talent over sales and underground respect over mainstream success. After the label's first two official releases – the debut projects by Heltah Skeltah (*Nocturnal*) and Originoo Gunn Clappaz (*Da Storm*) – Duck Down's four original acts had each released an album by 1997. In an effort to raise the profile of both the label and the individual acts, the four groups formed a collective known as Boot Camp Clik and released a project of their own that same year entitled *For the People*. Boot Camp would come to epitomize the entire Duck Down movement – well-respected and critically acclaimed music that did not top the charts but gained a loyal, cult-like following of fans that would pack small venues for raucous live shows. In recent years, the label has expanded to include younger and more diverse artists such as Kidz In The Hall and Skyzoo, as well as established veteran acts like Black Rob and Pharoahe Monch to compliment the original members. Instead of fading away like so many of its contemporaries, the label does not appear to be going anywhere. Over the course of Duck Down's history it has released more than 40 albums, totaling in over three million copies sold, but selling records was never the ultimate goal. Rather, it was founded as a way to distribute its artists' music to the public without having to compromise creative integrity. In that regard, Duck Down has been more than successful.

8. Tommy Boy Records

When I was first compiling this list I had a feeling that I was omitting a label, but I couldn't remember which one. That, in a nutshell, perfectly encapsulates **Tommy Boy Records**. Perhaps it was due to its artists not shouting it out in every song or the label's logo not being worn as a necklace, but for all of its success, Tommy Boy was a famous label that always seemed to be forgotten. Founded in 1981 by writer Tom Silverman, Tommy Boy boasted a much stronger roster of artists than many people may realize and was an influential entity during hip-hop's rise in the '80s and '90s. With a lineup that ranged from the Force MD's and Digital Underground to Coolio, and Stetsasonic, the label seemed to always have a new artist that appealed to the constantly changing tastes of fickle hip-hop fans. In the early '90s, two groups – House of Pain and Naughty by Nature – brought a darker and more intense vibe that was an interesting balance to some of the label's lighter offerings. Furthermore, the label was also the launching point for a member of hip-hop royalty, Queen Latifah, who was known as one of the nicest female emcees around and her first two albums, *All Hail the Queen* and *Nature of a Sista*, were released by Tommy Boy. Similarly, De La Soul, one of the most creative groups ever seen in hip-hop, brought even more respect and attention to its label, particularly through the release of their first two classic albums, *3 Feet High and Rising* and *De La Soul Is Dead*. Tommy Boy is no longer the independent powerhouse it once was and perhaps many people may forget its impact, but the influential groups and classic material that came out of the label are part of hip-hop lore and can never be forgotten.

7. Loud Records

Loud Records was founded in 1992 by Steve Rifkind, a record promoter and artist manager, as an offshoot of Rifkind's marketing company. While it lasted for only ten years before folding in 2002, it was a very significant decade for hip-hop and Loud was a major reason for it. At its apex, Loud's roster boasted some of the most talented acts in hip-hop and, most impressively, geography was not a factor. While many labels at the time were almost completely comprised of artists from one region of the country, Loud's artists came from all over the map, such as Los Angeles-based artists Xzibit and Tha Alkaholiks, Chicago-based Twista, and Three 6 Mafia, the Academy Award-winning group hailing from Memphis, Tennessee. At its core, however, Loud was a New York label anchored by New York artists. In 1993, the fledgling label released the Wu-Tang Clan's groundbreaking debut, *Enter the Wu-Tang [36 Chamber]*, followed by the group's next three albums, including their quadruple-platinum 1997 sophomore album, *Wu-Tang Forever*. In addition to the Clan, Loud's roster also included the critically and commercial successful duo Mobb Deep, Wu-Tang member Raekwon, and the first solo Latino emcee to go platinum, Big Punisher. Loud's influence extended beyond just the music. Rifkind is credited with being one of the originators of the concept of the "street team," an urban guerilla-style marketing campaign that promoted artists and albums by doing things such as handing out flyers outside of clubs and hanging up posters and stickers in well-traveled locations such as subway stations and bus stops. The label also changed the hip-hop music business when the Wu-Tang Clan signed its first contract. As a whole, the group was signed to Loud but it gave individual members the freedom to sign with any label of their choosing. It was an unprecedented deal that brought more attention to the members' solo projects, which in turn raised the entire group's profile and brought more sales to Loud. Such innovative business practices made Loud was one of hip-hop's strongest and most important labels.

6. Ruthless Records

The godfather of "gangster rap," Eazy-E, co-founded **Ruthless Records** in 1987 as a way to distribute the music he and his friends were making at the time. They formed a group called N.W.A and, in the process, changed the music business forever. In addition to Eazy, there were two songwriters – Ice Cube and MC Ren – and two producers – Dr. Dre and DJ Yella – that, collectively, comprised the self-proclaimed "world's most dangerous group." The label's first two efforts, N.W.A's debut *Straight Outta Compton* and Eazy-E's initial solo album, *Eazy-Duz-It*, were released within a month of one another in 1988 and both reached double-platinum status while giving birth to the subgenre of "gangster rap." The success of the albums becomes even more impressive when considering that Ruthless was able to accomplish this without any either album receiving significant radio or video airplay. In reality, Ruthless was the first hip-hop label that was based on word-of-mouth promotion (not to mention the media attention that came from receiving a letter of criticism from an assistant director of the FBI). The following year, the label would release the solo album of Dr. Dre's protégé, The D.O.C., to widespread critical acclaim. N.W.A would disband in 1991 after releasing an EP and a second album, both platinum, and many believed that Ruthless would soon fold, but that would not be the case. On top of Eazy's own successful career (he sold over 6 million records as a solo artist), Ruthless became home to one of the most successful musical acts of the decade. Bone Thugs-n-Harmony released five albums on the label, all of which reached platinum status and sold a total of more than 16 million copies combined. Additionally,

their single "Tha Crossroads," the group's tribute to Eazy, sold two million copies of its own and won a Grammy award for "Best Rap Performance by a Duo or Group." While Eazy-E's death in 1995 effectively shut down Ruthless less than 10 years after its inception, the label's impact will continue to be felt for years to come. Without Ruthless, hip-hop would not be nearly the worldwide cultural phenomenon that it is today.

5. Aftermath Entertainment

Aftermath Entertainment, the label Dr. Dre founded after leaving Death Row Records, appeared to be a flop initially. The label's first two releases – *Dr. Dre Presents the Aftermath*, a compilation showcasing the label's roster of artists, the vast majority of which (Hands-On, Who'z Who, Nowl, etc.) were complete unknowns to the general public, and *The Firm: The Album*, the first and only offering from the Nas-led supergroup of the same name – were major disappointments. Both albums sold over a million copies each, but were critically panned and ultimately considered failures. It looked as if Dre's decision to create his own imprint would mean the end of his career. However, Dr. Dre – and, by extension, Aftermath – would soon find a very unlikely savior: a white rapper. Eminem's debut album, *The Slim Shady LP* went four-times platinum when it was released in early 1999. Later that same year, Dre himself released his long awaited sophomore album, *2001*, which itself sold over 6 million records. At the same time, virtually all of the artists that had been featured on *Dr. Dre Presents the Aftermath* were released from the label as the signing of Eminem started to change the direction of the label, including the signing of Eminem's protégé, 50 Cent, who signed a joint record that was split between Aftermath and Eminem's own label, **Shady Records**. Proportionally, Aftermath Entertainment is arguably the most successful label in history. There have been a total of 18 LP's released under the Aftermath banner and only one, *Truthfully Speaking* by R&B singer Truth Hurts, failed to sell 500,000 copies. Three more were certified gold but fell short of the one million sold plateau. The remaining 14 all reached platinum status and two, *The Marshall Mathers LP* and *The Eminem Show*, both by Eminem, were certified diamond, signifying more than ten million copies sold. Furthermore, all but two of the albums released on the label reached the top five of the *Billboard* 200 chart, with eleven going all the way to number one. Additionally, Eminem was named the best-selling artist of the decade by Nielsen SoundScan with over 32 million copies sold from 2000 – 2009. Considering Dr. Dre's ability to find new artists, not to mention his well-documented perfectionism, it's hard to bet against the continued success of Aftermath.

4. Cold Chillin' Records

With a roster that resembled an all-star team from the golden age of hip-hop, **Cold Chillin' Records** was one of the genre's most influential record labels of the late '80s. While it lasted for less than a decade after its launch in 1986, Cold Chillin' released several classic albums from some of hip-hop's biggest stars and pioneered trends that continue to thrive today. Cold Chillin's artists, the majority of whom were collectively known as the "Juice Crew," were anchored by producer Marley Marl and they are credited with popularizing the concept of the answer record – responding to a perceived slight in a song with a retaliatory song of their own. The Juice Crew included some of the most significant and ground-breaking New York artists of the decade, including all-time greats such as MC Shan, Biz Markie, Big Daddy Kane, and Kool G. Rap. Much of today's hip-hop can be traced back to Cold Chillin' in one way or another. First, producers such as Pete Rock and DJ Premier cite Marley Marl has a major influence on their own musical development. Secondly, "Roxanne's Revenge," by Roxanne Shanté was not only a major breakthrough for female emcees, but also one of the first answer records to become famous. Next, "The Symphony," billed as Marley Marl featuring Masta Ace, Craig G., Kool G. Rap & Big Daddy Kane," is still considered to be the model posse cut in hip-hop history and has spawned reinterpretations from artists as varied as EPMD and Master P. Finally, MC Shan's "The Bridge," which would prompt a response, "South Bronx," from KRS-One's Boogie Down Productions, kicked off a series of songs that would ultimately become known as the "Bridge Wars" that is considered a classic hip-hop rivalry that elevated the genre and brought mainstream attention to the (non-violent) competition aspect of the music. The start of a new decade signaled a new direction for hip-hop and Cold Chillin' had trouble adapting. By 1994, it had become overshadowed by new labels such as Death Row and Bad Boy and it would effectively close up shop a year later, but the label's importance is impossible to ignore.

3. Death Row Records

The rise and fall of **Death Row Records**, the most controversial record label in the history of American music, could fill an entire book all on its own. Co-founded in 1991 by Dr. Dre, fresh from his departure from N.W.A and Ruthless Records, and a former bodyguard named Marion "Suge" Knight, Death Row dominated hip-hop for four years, starting with the label's first release, Dr. Dre's *The Chronic*, in 1992 and lasting until the Tupac Shakur's death in 1996. What Death Row lacked in longevity, it more than made up for in swagger, controversy and, of course, music. Dr. Dre's first post-N.W.A song was the title track to the soundtrack for the film *Deep Cover*. In addition to establishing Dre as a solo artist, it also introduced a future superstar named Snoop Doggy Dogg and laid the foundation for Dre's debut album. Featuring the label's roster of artists – Snoop, Tha Dogg Pound, Nate Dogg, RBX, and The Lady of Rage – known collectively as the "Death Row Inmates," *The Chronic* was both a critical and commercial success, selling over three million copies, and immediately establishing Death Row as a legitimate label as well as introducing a new sound called "G-Funk." It was only the beginning. From November, 1993 – November, 1996, Death Row released seven more projects – five albums (two by Snoop Doggy Dogg, two by 2Pac, and one by Tha Dogg Pound) and two soundtracks (*Above The Rim* and *Murder Was The Case*). Six reached the top spot on the *Billboard* 200 – the other one reached number two – and together they sold more than 31 million copies. It would not last. To escape Knight's tyrannical ways, Dr. Dre left to start Aftermath in 1996, mere months before the murder of Shakur. Despite the occasional success, mostly posthumous 2Pac releases, Death Row's reign ended only four short years after it began, but at its peak the label truly was untouchable.

2. Bad Boy Records

When Sean Combs was fired from his position at Uptown Records, he was probably the only person that believed it would actually help his career. But that's precisely what happened when Combs founded **Bad Boy Records** and changed the future of hip-hop in the process. In addition to signifying the label's inception, Bad Boy's first album, released on September 13, 1994, also gave birth to the short but unforgettable career of a new rap star named Christopher Wallace. *Ready to Die* introduced The Notorious B.I.G. to the world and, just one week later, the label introduced Craig Mack with his own debut, *Project: Funk da World*. Combs also knew how to cross-promote, being the first to feature his R&B acts on his rappers' songs and vice versa as a way to expand hits artists' visibility. As a result, it quickly became evident that the fledgling label was a force to be reckoned with. After dropping only three albums – all R&B, all platinum – over the next two years, Bad Boy completely dominated hip-hop with three releases in 1997 – B.I.G.'s sophomore effort, *Life After Death*, Combs' own debut (as Puff Daddy), *No Way Out*, and newcomer Mase's first album, *Harlem World*. Each of the three reached number one on the *Billboard* 200 and combined to sell more than 21 million copies in the United Sates alone. Of course, Wallace's murder two weeks before his second album's release made the success bittersweet. Since then, as the music climate became more crowded, Bad Boy began to release more material in an effort to diversify while Combs himself focused on a myriad of other ventures. Overall, Bad Boy has 27 platinum and 13 gold plaques to its credit and while it peaked a decade-and-a-half ago, it's obvious that they won't stop.

1. Def Jam Recordings

After nearly thirty years of setting the tone for the entire genre, **Def Jam Recordings** is undoubtedly the greatest record label in hip-hop history. The home that Rick Rubin and Russell Simmons built (and Lyor Cohen later took over) continues to reinvent itself every few years, steadily cranking out hits and introducing dozens of stars to the music world since the mid-'80s. LL Cool J's 1985 debut, *Radio*, and the Beastie Boys' classic first album, *Licensed to Ill*, released a year later, kicked off Def Jam's reign. Over the next ten years, seminal artists such as Public Enemy, Slick Rick, 3rd Base, EPMD, Redman, Onyx, Method Man, Warren G, and Foxy Brown would all release classic material on the label. Towards the end of the

90's, after falling a bit behind upstarts Death Row and Bad Boy, Def Jam experienced a commercially successful renaissance behind newcomer DMX. Plus, joint ventures with Murder Inc. and Roc-A-Fella Records brought Ja Rule and Jay-Z (and eventually Kanye West) under the label's umbrella. More recently, Def Jam has acquired hip-hop legends Nas, Ghostface Killah, and The Roots to go with Rick Ross, Young Jeezy, Fabolous, and their other emerging stars. Unlike virtually every other hip-hop label, Def Jam has persevered, through lean times and various regime changes, including a power struggle that left label co-founder Rick Rubin out, not to mention a stint with none other than Jay-Z serving as president. Through it all, Def Jam has remained atop the genre, with 80 gold and platinum albums and more than 45 million copies sold in the United States alone. In late 2011, authors Bill Adler and Dan Charnas published a book on the label calling it the "last great record label." When looking at its history as well as its impact on the music industry, it's a description that is tough to dispute.

Honorable Mentions

Rap-A-Lot Records

Roc-A-Fella Records

Cash Money Records

THE HIP-HOP 10

9. THE MOST UNDERRATED ARTISTS OF ALL TIME

10. Nature

A protégé of Nas, **Nature** appeared destined for greatness and stardom, becoming known to many after replacing Cormega as a member of the supergroup The Firm in 1997. Despite the group's disappointing outcome, Nature became renowned as an artist to be respected and fans geared up for his album. In September, 2000, he finally released his major label debut, *For All Seasons*, to strong critical reviews. On "We Ain't Friends" he analyzed the deterioration of a tight friendship from the inside: *"Do the math, yo, add and subtract/Every year I lose a close friend/Too many haven't come back/I seen niggas on the night of their death/I sat in on niggas baggin' up/Going home, inspired the chef/I tried to make a little money, dun, and buy it myself/Not knowing that this drug shit required some help/I had nowhere to turn, yo, what could I do?/When you gave me your back like, 'Nigga, Fuck you!'"* However, when the album didn't sell, Nature was dropped from his record deal and his relationship with Nas soured, a case of life imitating art. Nature's skills were never an issue and it's amazing to think what would have happened if that first album had turned a profit.

9. Jeru The Damaja

In response to the ever-growing trend in the mid-1990s of rappers that claimed to be crime bosses in their music came **Jeru The Damaja**, an emcee whose music focused on reality and truth rather than grandiose mobster ambitions. This approach was best explored in the song that was directed at what Jeru believed to be wanna-be tough guys and studio gangsters, "Ya Playin' Yaself": *"The race is on/But I won't compete in this competition/Because I have a greater mission/I hope that you listen/Knowledge, wisdom, and understanding brings long life and health/Think anything else and ya playin' yaself."* Sometimes, however, the music can overshadow the lyrics and part of the reason Jeru's first two albums, *The Sun Rises in the East* and *Wrath of the Math*, received critical acclaim was DJ Premier's terrific production. The two decided to part ways after Jeru's second album and the rapper's visibility faded. His skills, meanwhile, remained top notch and, no matter who is crafting the beats, Jeru's lyrics make him one of the genre's most underappreciated artists.

8. Cormega

When Nas introduced The Firm on the song "Affirmative Action" on his sophomore album *It Was Written*, a verse from a little-known rapper named **Cormega** caught the attention of everyone. Unfortunately, that would signal the pinnacle of his prominence as he would be kicked out of The Firm shortly thereafter and dropped from Def Jam Recording without releasing an album on the label. Despite the setbacks, 'Mega persevered, releasing six independent albums and becoming one of the stalwarts of the underground thanks to songs like "American Beauty": *"You know the wisdom is reflected in the knowledge when it's manifested/If not fed in due time, the mind is anorexic/You understand the message/I know I'm getting too deep for some/Rhyme, uncut raw, the beat numb."* Cormega may have missed his opportunity to become a star, but no one can deny his impact on the music and his standing amongst the other lyrical giants of his time.

7. Styles P

When most people think of The LOX, they first think of Jadakiss, but it's his rhyme partner, **Styles P**, that deserves just as much attention and praise. Unfortunately, the qualities that make Styles great are the same qualities that make him unappreciated among the general public. Self-proclaimed as the "hardest rapper out," he never compromised his lyrics or reached for a larger, mainstream audience. In fact, the first single off his debut solo album, "Good Times," was about smoking marijuana and employed a chorus that was a sample of Freda Payne's 1976 single, "I Get High (On Your Memory)." Such a song is fitting for an artist like Styles, who once said: *"You heard it from the P, you ought to know it's the truth/I'll get you kidnapped and raped and thrown off a roof/You could nod your head to this like it's only a rap/'cause when these bullets hit your ass I'm like, 'It's only a gat'/I need a funeral to feel good, I'm hoping it's yours/Think he's religious? Heard he got shot in the cross/Holiday Styles, bitch I broke most of the laws."* With such raw imagery, it's not hard to see why most people have never heard of Styles P. It's also not hard to see why he deserves to be heard by as many people as possible.

6. Sean Price

Sometimes the success of a group can overshadow the abilities of its individual members, leading the public to think of the artists involved only in terms of the collective. This is certainly the case with Boot Camp Clik and its oft-unheralded wordsmith, **Sean Price**. Originally known as Ruck when he came upon the scene as one-half of the Brooklyn duo Heltah Skeltah, Price's verses are a lethal combination of introspective lyrics, funny punchlines, and in-your-face aggression and bravado. On "Figure Four," he boasts: *"Too old to rap, too young to wack/10 fingers, two hands/My nigga, the guns clap/I don't like niggas no more/eight-figure dreams, nigga, but the figure is four/These are words from a* *thousandaire/Selling crack in the P's disguised in some housing gear/I fucked up somewhere/Down the line/But I got my shit in order/The crown is mine.*" Sean Price may never be bigger than his group, but much of what makes Boot Camp legendary is found within him.

5. Immortal Technique

The most politically charged emcee since Public Enemy's Chuck D, **Immortal Technique** uses his position as an artist to shine a light on concerns that affect downtrodden individuals within urban areas, as well as major issues on the world stage. With album titles such as *Revolutionary, The 3rd World,* and *The Martyr*, Technique's subject matter and focus is obvious and further reinforced with honest and emotional lines like, "*My mother told me that placing my faith in God was the answer/But then I hated God 'cause he gave my mother cancer/Killing us slow like the Feds did to the Black Panthers.*" Immortal Technique speaks truth to power and everyone could benefit from hearing that truth.

4. Masta Ace

Eminem has said that **Masta Ace** made him want to rap and it's doubtful he is the only one that feels that way. A member of the legendary Juice Crew, Ace ultimately became disillusioned with the increasingly commercial reach of hip-hop artists and preferred instead to remain unknown and release music that remained true to his artistic vision. Amazingly, he made his recording debut on the classic posse cut, "The Symphony," with a line that became a mantra in hip-hop: "*There's a sign at the door: 'No Bitin' Allowed.'*" While he never received the mainstream popularity of fellow members Kool G. Rap or Big Daddy Kane, Ace continued to receive plenty of attention and acclaim within hip-hop's underground scene. It's the way he preferred it, but in doing so, he deprived millions of fans from realizing his greatness.

3. Treach

Best known for early-'90s party anthems, Naughty By Nature front man **Treach** has been overlooked since the beginning of his career. While the group experienced commercial success with hits like "O.P.P." and "Hip Hop Hooray," the catchy hooks and dance-friendly beats often took the attention away from the witty wordplay and breathless flow that Treach displayed, best exemplified on "Feel Me Flow," another Naughty hit: *"The flow pro poetical/With skills only a vet will know/Better know/Where's the wetter flow/That's on point like decimals."* Naughty By Nature sold millions of records and even won a Grammy, but somehow its vocal leader continues to fly under the radar.

2. AZ

Trying to explain why **AZ** is not as well-known or revered as his contemporaries Nas, Raekwon and The Notorious B.I.G. is an almost impossible task. The only artist featured on Nas's classic debut *Illmatic*, AZ appeared to be next in line to help return New York to the forefront of the music, but his own stellar debut, 1995's *Doe or Die*, failed to make much of a commercial impact and he was immediately considered a disappointment by many. Quietly, though, AZ has put together an almost twenty-year career and has released eight albums, each full of dense lyrical content and vivid imagery, like in "Rather Unique": *"My verbals rip shit/Brains give birth to thoughts in triplets/Fuck it, I'm on some flip shit/Ready to let my clip spit/Dramatical/Vocals release shells like automatics through musics/Magical/Causing any battles to be tragical, child/Got a style sick as Hell/Sicker than sickle cell anemia/Slaughter your circulatory like Leukemia."* AZ may have never reached his potential in terms of stardom and records sold, but his music has always been top notch.

1. Black Thought

The front man and co-founder of The Roots, **Black Thought** is easily the most underrated artist in hip-hop history. The favorite rapper of Big Pun, Thought has been delivering a combination of thought-provoking and uplifting, yet brutally honest, rhymes over his group's live instrumentation since the early 1990's, best exemplified on 2008's "75 Bars (Black's Reconstruction)": *"I'm a modern day saint/I'm a modern day Kane/My definition, I can finally explain/Cold, smooth like that dude Sean Connery was playing/I just got to be the man/I'm the father figure and/When I spit, it's something like a psychology exam/If you stand where I stood, you could probably understand/How the mic's feeling like a million dollars in my hand/It's the* Silence of the Lambs/*Go and cop another gram*." With a live show that is considered to be one of the best in the world, Black Thought's brilliance extends far beyond the studio and while The Roots often receive their deserved recognition, its main voice remains an unknown to the larger masses, an act that should be considered a crime in the music world.

Honorable Mentions

Inspectah Deck

Spice-1

Posdnuous

8. THE BIGGEST BUSTS OF ALL TIME

10. Cory Gunz

The son of a platinum-selling rapper (Peter Gunz), **Cory Gunz**, is a hip-hop legacy and was essentially born with a microphone in his hand. The junior Gunz has been coveted by the biggest labels in the industry but, despite being initially signed to Def Jam before moving on to Young Money Entertainment, still has not yet released an actual album. With his rapid-fire delivery, breathless flow, and clever lines like, *"Psychologically, so illogical/By mythology, I'm catastrophically philosophical/They're isosceles,"* Cory Gunz may still have a very successful career but, at this point, he can only be considered a disappointment.

9. Cassidy

One of the most anticipated artists of the early 2000's, **Cassidy** was the anchor of producer Swizz Beatz's fledgling Full Service Records. Known for his clever punchlines, Cass became famous overnight after defeating Roc-A-Fella upstart Freeway in a freestyle battle by a unanimous decision from the judges. His first album, 2004's *Split Personality*, reached number 2 on the *Billboard* 200 chart and sold over 500,000 copies, but was a disappointment to both fans and critics. His next effort, *I'm a Hustla*, was released a year later and debuted at the top of the charts but, despite a single that sold over a million ringtones, the album failed to even go gold and Cassidy was considered a disappointment. His next two albums would also flop and Cassidy was written off for good. With metaphors and similes like, *"Go ahead and tell your boys to try me/My trigger finger itching like it's got poison ivy,"* Cassidy will be remembered as one of the biggest what-ifs in hip-hop lore.

8. Da Band

When Sean "Diddy" Combs decided to hold an open audition to find the next act for Bad Boy Records and film the endeavor for an MTV reality show, over 40,000 aspiring artists applied. Combs chose six artists – four emcees, an R&B singer, and a reggae artist – to form a group that would ultimately become known as **Da Band**. It didn't work out as planned for Chopper, Babs, Ness, Freddy P, Sara, and Dylan. The group's sole release, *Too Hot for T.V.*, reached gold status, but the experiment was an unmitigated failure. While the show was intended to introduce the unit to the public, it was actually the most attention the group would receive and Combs dissolved the collective shortly after the album dropped. It was the wise move. After all, when a group is most famous for walking from Midtown Manhattan to Brooklyn to retrieve a slice of Junior's Cheesecake, disbanding is probably the best approach.

7. Memphis Bleek

The longtime heir to the Roc-A-Fella throne, **Memphis Bleek** has been Jay-Z's successor for more than a decade, but he's never been able to step up to the next level. While all four of his albums have been certified gold, Jay-Z, not to mention the public at large, expected so much more. There have been times when the hype has been warranted, like when Bleek stole the show from Amil, Beanie Sigel, and even Jay himself, on the posse cut "4 Da Fam": *"Straight from the borough of them B.K. niggas/Where we rob for the fun of it, hustle for the drug of it/Wrap money in rubber bands just* *for the love it/Straight from my ghetto, we listen to heavy metal/Like/desert eagles, street sweepers, loud metal/It's hit and run now, motherfuck any one of you/We them niggas be in your crib just like furniture.*" Regrettably for Bleek, that type of performance has been more of the exception rather than the rule and the hip-hop community has accepted the fact that the crown just doesn't seem to fit on Bleek's head. When Jay-Z famously rhymed, "*Bleek can be one hit away his whole career/As long as I'm alive, he's a millionaire/And even if I die, he's in my will somewhere,*" it appeared that he finally accepted it too.

6. Craig G

The Juice Crew was hip-hop's first all-star team and "The Symphony" was their magnum opus. The second emcee heard on the track went by the name of **Craig G** and he held his own with the other three hip-hop heavyweights with a verse that had fans eagerly anticipating his solo effort: "*That's how I'm living – all surprise mode/Don't even sleep, try not to keep your eyes closed/'Cause if you do, when you awaken/Your so-called spot will be taken/I'll take you over like a greedy executive/'Cause on the mic my perspective is/To be the best in all rap events, and since I have a call, I call experience.*" The anticipation, however, was wasted when Craig G finally released his debut, *The Kingpin*, led by a hip-house single, "Turn This House Into a Home," both of which flopped. Although he kept his skills, Craig G's reputation would never recover and "The Symphony" would forever remain the pinnacle of his career.

5. Saigon

Sometimes even being featured on a hit television show isn't enough to give an artist the necessary spark to become a star. When underground favorite **Saigon** appeared in four episodes of *Entourage* in 2005, it seemed to be the perfect springboard to his forthcoming debut, *The Greatest Story Never Told*. However, due to numerous setbacks, the album was not released until 2011, long after Sai's buzz had fizzled and other new artists had emerged on the scene to take his place. It was a missed opportunity. Saigon had all the necessary tools and his duet with the legendary Kool G. Rap, the alliteration-heavy, "The Letter P," showcased his talents exquisitely: *"Please, people ain't prepared to be persuaded by political paraphrases they printing in the papers/I'm positioning my peers to pump-pump/Put the pound to the pig, just let them pump-pump/I pause for you people to peep the letter P/Poetically put the paragraph so perfectly."* It's difficult not to wonder how drastically different Saigon's career would have been if his debut LP had never been delayed back in 2006.

4. The Firm

It may seem counterintuitive to label a platinum-selling group as a flop but for **The Firm**, one million records sold was considered a starting point, not a final destination. The Nas-helmed supergroup that included AZ, Foxy Brown, and Nature, decided to go for broke by tapping superproducers Dr. Dre and Trackmasters to co-produce their debut album. The result was a disjointed effort with schizophrenic beats and so many guest artists that it resembled a compilation rather than a singularly focused effort and it was almost universally panned by critics and fans alike. As a result, The Firm would never recover. In fact, the album was such a disappointment that the group disbanded and has never (yet) reunited.

3. Shyne

The target of a bidding war between Bad Boy and Def Jam in 1998, **Shyne** sounded like a replica of The Notorious B.I.G. and was expected to fill the late great emcee's considerable shoes. While his eponymous debut album would eventually reach platinum status, its release was overshadowed by the dark cloud of legal trouble hanging over his head. That trouble would eventually lead to a ten-year prison sentence and Shyne's once-promising career completely derailed. His first single, "Bad Boyz," proved he had to the skills to be a star – *"Bullets heat-seeking, street sweeping/With an evil grin/Watch you die, one love, one life, one Shyne/Y'all niggas ain't saying nothing/Like a mime"* – but enormous expectations and a life-changing mistake prevented Shyne from ever becoming the artist that mandated that initial bidding war.

2. Papoose

When legendary New York radio DJ Kay Slay introduced an up-and-coming Brooklyn emcee named **Papoose** in 2004, the hip-hop community immediately took notice. The following year, he delivered a scene-stealing verse on Busta Rhymes' star-studded "Touch It [Remix]," and won the *Justo Award* for Underground Rapper of the Year. Without a doubt, Pap's reputation was solidified on his song "Alphabet Slaughter," where he played alliteration with all 26 letters: *"(H!) Head hoodlum, hitting heads heavenly, hypnotizing/Hire hitmen harmlessly, holding heaters, hospitalizing/High-holding hammers, hectically hitting herbs, homiciding/Helicopter hijacking, holding hostages, horrifying."* A year after that, on the strength of fourteen solo mixtapes, the public was clamoring for Pap's LP, *The Nacirema Dream*, and Jive Records signed him to an unprecedented $1.5 million contract, outbidding all other labels. It turned out to be a poor investment: the artist and the label parted ways in 2007 without any material being released. As of early 2012, Papoose had still never released a full-length album.

1. Canibus

Arguably the most anticipated hip-hop artist in history, **Canibus** was expected to fill the void that had been left by the deaths of 2Pac and The Notorious B.I.G. By all accounts, he was the next in the long line of great emcees that would dominate the genre for several years and bless the world with classic albums that would never sound dated. After many jaw-dropping guest appearances and numerous vicious freestyles that featured his signature sound of a gruff voice presenting picturesque lyrics, historical metaphors, and elaborate rhyme schemes in an effortless flow and perfect cadence, Canibus was seen as a sure thing. Rhymes such as, *"Ambushing emcees/Jumping out the trees/Like Vietnamese/In fatigues/Covered in leaves,"* and *"I'll attack you with words that's absurd/And rip your fucking skin off just to get on your nerves,"* had everyone anticipating his album. When the album, the Wyclef Jean-produced *Can-I-Bus*, finally did arrive in September, 1998, it landed with a thud, disappointing everyone that heard it and forever branding Canibus as a bust. In the years since, Canibus has released more than ten solo albums and been a part of several collaborations, including as one-half of The Undergods with Keith Murray and as a quarter of the supergroup The Four Horsemen with Kurupt, Killah Priest, and Ras Kass. It didn't matter. The legacy of Canibus was cemented following the disappointment of that debut album and there was almost nothing that could be done to change it. From a technical standpoint, Canibus is one of the most gifted rappers to ever enter a studio and, as such, his lack of critical and commercial success makes him the most disappointing hip-hop artist in history.

Honorable Mentions

Consequence

Asher Roth

Charles Hamilton

THE HIP-HOP 10

7. THE BEST SONGS OF ALL TIME

10. "Hard Knock Life (Ghetto Anthem)" – Jay-Z (1998)

After the death of his friend The Notorious B.I.G., Jay-Z was initially going to name his second album *Heir to the Throne, vol. 1* but wisely chose to name it *In My Lifetime, vol. 1* instead. While a modest commercial success, ultimately reaching platinum status, it was an uneven effort and it certainly did not convince anyone that he would be the next king of hip-hop. That would change the following year thanks to a sample of a Broadway musical that featured children on the chorus: *"It's the hard knock life for us/It's the hard knock life for us/'Steada treated, we get tricked/'Steada kisses, we get kicked/It's the had knock life."* Nominated for a Grammy, **"Hard Knock Life (Ghetto Anthem)"** was Jay-Z's first big hit, and catapulted *Vol. 2...Hard Knock Life* to the top spot on the *Billboard* 200, his first album to reach number one. The song is a study in contradictions. The drumbeat itself is slow and methodical, but the keys are fast and almost frantic. Similarly, the loop of the kids singing the chorus belies the harsh reality within Jay's lyrics: *"We live in hard knocks/We don't take over, we borrow blocks/Burn 'em down and you can have it back, daddy..."* Although "Empire State of Mind" is Jay-Z's biggest hit, "Hard Knock Life (Ghetto Anthem)" is his most important and, all things considered, the best single in the Brooklyn legend's extensive catalogue.

9. "Top Billin'" – Audio Two (1987)

In hip-hop, imitation really is the most sincere form of flattery. While Masta Ace proclaimed that biting was not allowed, it has now become commonplace for an artist to pay homage by borrowing lines from a classic song. There are a handful of songs that have helped to build the foundation of the music and, as a result, have been quoted repeatedly. Audio Two's "**Top Billin'**" is one of those songs. Dr. Dre, The Notorious B.I.G., 2Pac, AZ, Wyclef Jean, 50 Cent, and many others have sampled or referenced "Top Billin'" in their own songs, proving how significant it is, even to this day. While not a traditional chorus, the song had a refrain that strung the verses together without breaking the flow: *"Milk is chillin', Giz is chillin'/What more can I say? Top billin'/That's what we get, got it good/And since you understood…"* Milk Dee's lyrics, which were appreciated for their realness and honesty rather than their depth, became universally known thanks in part to his unique voice and crisp, direct flow, all of which make it the perfect song to sample. Although many younger fans are not aware of "Top Billin'" itself, anyone that has heard a hip-hop song on the radio in the past twenty years has heard some type of allusion to it, making "Top Billin'" that much more important.

8. "Stan" – Eminem (2000)

Following the surprising success of his first album, *The Slim Shady LP*, Eminem came under fire from activist groups for lyrics that were deemed misogynistic, homophobic, and many other things. When his highly anticipated sophomore album, *The Marshall Mathers LP*, dropped, fans expected much of the same. Their expectations were not only met, but exceeded, as Em upped the ante in every conceivable way, seemingly trying to offend anyone he didn't piss off the first time. But the album's gem was a song that most detractors never thought an artist like Eminem could ever conceive. "**Stan**," a song that had Eminem acting as an increasingly desperate obsessive fan for the first three verses before responding to the fan as himself, was a direct result of Em's overnight superstardom. Accounts vary as to whether the song was based on one specific fan or an amalgamation of many, but the basis of the track does not change its brilliance. The genius of "Stan" is two-fold. First is the way in which the story builds – Stan is more agitated with each verse, becoming louder and angrier, expressing his frustrations to his hero as the sound of a scribbling pencil can be heard underneath the lyrics. For example, early on, he first blames the lack of response on his poor handwriting, saying, *"Sometimes I scribble addresses too sloppy when I jot 'em,"* but in the third verse the blame shifts to the artist: *"I know you got my last two letters, I wrote the addresses on them perfect."* Secondly, the song ultimately works because of the honesty that is contained within the storytelling, which is only possible because Eminem has been on both sides of this conversation – he was once the superfan with a pregnant girlfriend and no money and he's now the focus of worldwide adulation. In his response, Em also nods to all of the people that called him the antichrist and admits that he's playing with all of us: *"But what's this shit you said about you like to cut your wrists too?/I say that shit just clowning, dog/C'mon, how fucked up is you?"* The ultimate proof of the song's power is the fact that the term "stan" has entered the lexicon to describe a blindly loyal, die-hard fan (Nas even used the term to describe Jay-Z in his vicious diss, "Ether"). Ironically, Eminem's song about an obsessed fan was so good that it helped propel the highest-selling album of his career and created an entire generation of stans.

7. "Dear Mama" – 2Pac (1995)

When 2Pac's third album, *Me Against The World*, was released in 1995, it marked the first time that an imprisoned artist had the number one LP on the *Billboard* 200 chart. The fact that the album's first single, "**Dear Mama**," was a heartfelt dedication to his mother perfectly illustrated the dichotomy that existed within 2Pac, a highly emotional artist. At times, that emotion got 'Pac into so much trouble that he wound up in prison; at other times, it led to the most insightful and passionate music of his career. "Dear Mama" is the epitome of the latter. In 1995, as the era of Mafioso rap was in full swing, the idea of an emcee rapping about how much he loved his mother was a risky decision that could have irreparably hurt his image (much like Mase's ill-fated feel good musical comeback in 2004). However, 2Pac was known to put raw emotion into his music and, more importantly, the song sounds great. The track starts with a subdued 2Pac saying, *"You are appreciated."* From there, Tony Pizarro's beat and the chorus by Reggie Green and Sweet Franklin bring a passionate ambiance that build upon 'Pac's honest lyrics. *"And I could see you coming home after work late/You're in the kitchen trying to fix us a hot plate/Just working with the scraps you was given/And mama made miracles every Thanksgiving/But now the road got rough, you're alone/You're trying to raise two bad kids on your own/And there's no way I can pay you back/But my plan is to show you that I understand/You are appreciated..."* After "Dear Mama," other artists such as Ghostface Killah, Canibus, Kanye West, Jay-Z and Snoop Dogg have made songs dedicated to their matriarchs. Too often in hip-hop, artists refuse to acknowledge their real lives before music so as not to undermine their person. 2Pac not only acknowledged his mother's influence on him, he embraced and broadcasted it, creating the best song of his life and giving other rappers the confidence to do the same.

6. "The Message" – Grandmaster Flash and the Furious Five (1982)

In 1982, the main focus of many hip-hop songs was still the music while the lyrics were secondary. This trend would change throughout the 1980s, starting with "**The Message**." While the song is credited to Grandmaster Flash and the Furious Five, the lyrics were written and performed almost exclusively by group member Melle Mel. The dark and authentic lyrical content was in stark contrast to the fun-loving party records that had dominated hip-hop until that point. It was a welcome change as the song sold over a million copies in less than a month. Mel's lyrics painted a bleak and hopeless picture, reflecting what many within inner cities were feeling as a result of Reaganomics and the sudden ubiquity of crack cocaine: *"Broken glass everywhere/People pissing on the stairs, you know they just don't care/I can't take the smell, can't take the noise/Got no money to move out, I guess I got no choice/Rats in the front room, roaches in the back/Junkies in the alley with a baseball bat/I tried to get away, but I couldn't get far/'cause a man with a tow truck repossessed my car..."* One of the first honest songs to be played on the radio, Melle Mel used the music as a mirror to reflect what he saw around him every day. Following "The Message," many artists began to make songs with blunter lyrics examining the plight of urban living rather than upbeat party records to escape that reality. The influence and legacy of the song continues to this day with Ice Cube, Puff Daddy, Snoop Dogg, Common, AZ, and many others quoting or referencing the song's lyrics. "The Message" was so important that it is the first hip-hop record to be included in the United States' National Recording Registry of historic sound recordings and is also a major reason that Grandmaster Flash and the Furious Five was the first hip-hop act inducted into the Rock and Roll Hall of Fame in 2007. Chuck D once called rap music the "Black CNN" and "The Message" was its first news story.

5. "Sraight Outta Compton" – N.W.A (1988)

The term "gangster rap" has been incorrectly used for nearly twenty years to describe virtually any hip-hop song that someone finds offensive or vulgar. In 1988, however, the term did not even exist until N.W.A burst onto the scene with "**Straight Outta Compton**," the lead single to their album of the same name. While another track from the album, "Fuck tha Police," would result in the group receiving a letter from the FBI and Secret Service denouncing the song, and also cement N.W.A's reputation as the "world's most dangerous group," it was "Straight Outta Compton" that would change hip-hop forever. When Dr. Dre proclaims, *"You are now about to witness the strength of street knowledge,"* at the start of the track, it is immediately clear that N.W.A is going to describe their surroundings, just as Melle Mel had done six years earlier. However, while "The Message" focused on life within New York City, "Straight Outta

Compton" described the lifestyles and issues of those living in South Central Los Angeles. The Dr. Dre and DJ Yella-produced track was loud and fast-paced, musically expressing all of the angst and anger felt by the young men, almost like a punch in the face sonically, but it still sounded crisp and polished, a perfect bed over which Ice Cube, MC Ren, and Eazy-E could vent their disillusionment. In fact, Cube's first verse would set the stage for the next half-decade of West Coast hip hop: *"Straight outta Compton, crazy motherfucker named Ice Cube/From the gang called Niggaz Wit Attitudes/When I'm called off, I got a sawed off/Squeeze the trigger and bodies are hauled off/You too, boy, if you fuck with me/The police are gonna have to come and get me/Off your ass/that's how I'm going out/For the punk motherfuckers that's showing out..."* The ultimate legacy of "Straight Outta Compton" was the introduction of not only N.W.A, but also the subgenre of "gangster rap," to the world at large

4. "Nuthin' But A 'G' Thang" – Dr. Dre (featuring Snoop Doggy Dogg) (1992)

Dr. Dre's solo debut, *The Chronic*, featuring raw lyrics over G-Funk instrumentals, forever changed the sound of hip-hop and established a new dynasty in rap. The album's first single, **"Nuthin' But A 'G' Thang**,*"* reintroduced Dre as a much more laidback solo artist and made 21 year-old newcomer Snoop Doggy Dogg into an overnight star. Much like Audio Two's "Top Billin'," it does not employ a traditional chorus, but rather a simple repeated refrain: *"It's like this, and like that, and like this, and uh/It's like that and like this, and like that, and uh/It's like this –/And who gives a fuck about hoes?/So just chill, 'til the next episode..."* The lyrics were more fun than insightful (*"Getting funky on the mic like an old batch of collard greens"*) and the beat was smooth and melodic, marking a drastic change from the violent fury and high-octane music of Dre's N.W.A days. "Nuthin' But A 'G' Thang" was a turning point for the genre, introducing "G-Funk," leading the transition of West Coast hip-hop to a much more relaxed vibe, and laying the foundation for Death Row's dominance over the next several years.

3. "Rapper's Delight" – The Sugarhill Gang (1979)

In the early days of hip-hop, the music was dominated by DJ's playing bouncy beats that allowed the crowd to dance. From there, the first emcees gave voice to the music, leading the party and often engaging the crowd in call-and-response chants. Freestyling and ciphers came soon after, but these new rappers were reluctant to put their voices on record. However, hip-hop pioneer Sylvia Robinson found three aspiring emcees that were willing to lend their voice to tape and decided to form them into a group called The Sugarhill Gang to record a song called "**Rapper's Delight**." While the song's lyrics were a bit pedestrian and delivered in a sing-song format, the track would break down barriers, becoming the first hip-hop song to become a Top 40 hit in the United States (36th on the *Billboard* Hot 100) and introducing the genre of hip-hop to the rest of the country and eventually the world. The opening hook, "*I said a hip, hop, the hippie the hippie/To the hip, hip, hop, a you don't stop/The rock it to the bang, bang boogie say "Up jumped the boogie!"/To the rhythm of the boogie, the beat…*" is one of the most famous refrains in hip-hop, not to mention music, history. While it hasn't aged particularly well and may seem harmless and even a bit corny when compared to the contributions of N.W.A and Public Enemy, "Rapper's Delight" paved the way for every song that followed and actually gave an initial identity to the embryonic genre. Sugarhill Gang helped to make it all possible.

2. "Fight the Power" – Public Enemy (1989)

In 1989, Spike Lee's critically acclaimed film *Do the Right Thing* told the story of escalating racial problems within a Brooklyn neighborhood. For the lead song for the soundtrack, Lee tapped the most intelligent, consciously aware group in hip-hop, Public Enemy, and they delivered with "**Fight the Power**." After releasing two albums, including the groundbreaking classic *It Takes a Nation of Millions to Hold Us Back*, P.E. was at the forefront of the politically-conscious, rebellious, pro-Black movement in hip-hop that included groups such as X-Clan and artists like KRS-One. On the other side of the coast, N.W.A was railing against the same issues, just in a different way. Both Public Enemy and N.W.A took the sentiments expressed in "The Message" a step further, but while N.W.A trained its animosity on the local forces that they felt were acting against them, P.E. spoke truth to power at a national level. With that in mind, it was a no brainer for them to lead the soundtrack to a film that would be tackling such strong subject matter. The result was four minutes and forty-two seconds of controlled musical fury. Over a multilayered track of loud drumbeats and various musical samples, vocalist Chuck D gave voice to a hopeless generation that had seen their neighborhoods disintegrate throughout the 1980s: *"From the heart/It's a start/A work of art/To revolutionize/Make a change/nothing's strange/People, people!/We are the same/No, we're not the same/'Cause we don't know the game/What we need is awareness/We can't get careless/You say, 'What is this?'/My beloved/Let's get down to business/Mental self-defensive fitness…"* Despite its strong message, the song was so good that it became a pop hit, reaching the top spot on the *Billboard* Hot Rap Singles chart. Over time, the legacy of "Fight the Power" has only grown as it was named the "greatest song of hip-hop" by VH1 and was included on prestigious lists such as the Rock and Roll Hall of Fame's "500 songs that Shaped Rock and Roll," *Rolling Stone*'s "500 Greatest Songs of All Time," AFI's "Songs of the Century," and *Time*'s "All-TIME 100 Songs." In essence, "Fight the Power" captured the emotions and attitudes of an entire generation in one song and while both Public Enemy and the subgenre that it spearheaded would fade out by the mid-'90s, the song's power and influence is still widely felt throughout the music industry.

1. "My Melody" – Eric B. & Rakim (1986)

It's not the most famous song on this list, but Eric B. & Rakim's "**My Melody**" is undoubtedly the most important. Without it, hip-hop would not have progressed so rapidly over the past 25 years and would not have reached the level that it has. In 1986, hip-hop was still defined more by its beats than its words and the vast majority of artists, including groundbreaking legends like Run-DMC, were spitting basic, single-rhyme lyrics that sound simplistic in retrospect. With "My Melody," Eric B. & Rakim flipped that construct, with Rakim delivering highly complex and multilayered verses over Eric B.'s stripped down beat that allowed the listener to focus on the words. With his dense lyrical content, relaxed style, and distinctive voice that sounded as if it had been filtered through a synthesizer, it almost seemed like Rakim was sent from the future or, at the very least, another planet. In reality, he was still in high school at the time and that fact makes this song even more impressive. When he says, *"My unusual style will confuse you a while,"* he is acknowledging that his method of rhyming had never been heard before and it may not be understood by all. Part of this confounding style was the wordplay that he employed, using double- and triple-timed rhymes ("unusual" rhymes with "confuse you," and "style" rhymes with "while") to create additional depth to his lyrics as he did when describing how his nickname of 'The R' seemed so natural: *"My name is Rakim Allah/And R. and A. stands for 'Ra'/Switch it around/It still comes out 'R.'"* While that rhyme may not seem all that impressive now, that type of verbal jousting had never been heard in hip-hop before Rakim arrived on the scene. In the mid-'80s, artists were not peppering their lyrics with double-entendres and metaphors the way they do now. Rakim is the reason for that growth. He threw down the gauntlet and challenged every other emcee, both at the time and those that would come after him, to step up their skills. That is what makes "My Melody" both great and important. When Rakim calmly rapped: *"I take 7 MC's, put 'em in a line/And add 7 more brothers who think they can rhyme/Well, it'll take 7 more before I go for mine/And that's 21 MC's ate up at the same time,"* he was both boasting about his skills and warning other rappers to meet his challenge. Both Nas and AZ, among many others, have cited those lines as the most influential on their careers. "My Melody" is chockfull of lines that have not only been sampled and quoted by artists, but also led to the development of some of the best emcees that have shaped hip-hop and pushed it forward over the past two decades. The impact of "My Melody" will continue to be felt for as long as hip-hop exists.

Honorable Mentions

"They Reminisce Over You (T.R.O.Y.)" – Pete Rock & CL Smooth (1992)

"Juicy" – The Notorious B.I.G. (1994)

"I Used To Love H.E.R." – Common (1994)

6. THE BEST REMIXES OF ALL TIME

10. "California Love" [Remix] – 2Pac (featuring Dr. Dre) (1996)

After Suge Kight paid $1.4 million to bail him out of jail, 2Pac immediately went to the studio and began working on his first album on Knight's Death Row Records, *All Eyez On Me*. Without question, the two most anticipated songs from that album were 'Pac's collaborations with Death Row's two biggest stars – "2 of Amerikaz Most Wanted" featuring Snoop Doggy Dogg and "**California Love**" featuring and produced by Dr. Dre. The latter was the album's first single, showcasing Dre and 'Pac each spitting a verse over a loud and relentless thumping beat. The album, however, only included the remix, a laid back and stripped down track that perfectly embodied mid-'90s West Coast hip-hop. While the verses are the same on both tracks, the rhymes and the flows that initially seemed tailor-made for the bombastic original actually sounded even better over the smooth rolling beat of the remix, particularly 2Pac's verse: *"It's west side, so you know the Row will bow down to no man/Say what you say/But give me that bomb beat from Dre/Let me serenade the streets of L.A./From Oakland to Sac-town/The Bay Area and back down/Cali is where they put they mack down/Give me love!"* While the original was a major hit that was embraced on the East Coast, the remix is the ultimate West Coast party track.

9. "Street Dreams" [Remix] – Nas (featuring R. Kelly) (1996)

The summer of 1996 was dominated by Nas and his sophomore album, *It Was Written*. While its first single, "If I Ruled The World (Imagine That)," was the biggest song of the summer, the album's second single, "**Street Dreams**," was also a major hit with a big budget *Casino*-inspired video directed by Hype Williams that matched the boisterous, up-tempo track. The remix could not have been any more different from the original as Nas calmly expounds over soft and slow piano chords: *"The black clouds over the hood/I'm on the corner with the thugs/Late night under the moon/As they assume I'm slanging drugs/'Cause I'm hooded up/Thought a G a night wasn't good enough/Pushed my luck/Yo, they had a brother put in cuffs/Luckily/Made it out of court comfortably/Judge said I need a job/Ain't nothing coming free."* R. Kelly's impassioned crooning on the chorus brings added emotional depth to the remix that was not present on the original.

8. "I Got 5 on It" [Remix] – Luniz (featuring Dru Down, E-40 Richie Rich, Shock G & Spice 1) (1995)

1995's "**I Got 5 on It**" was a West Coast anthem dedicated to hip-hop's favorite recreation that became a hit across the country. For the remix, The Luniz decided to recruit some veteran California heavyweights to rock over the instantly classic beat. While every featured artist brings his A-game, Shock G steals the show, switching from himself to his more famous alter ego, Humpty Hump, and then back: "[Shock G] *Yeah, it's been a while since I've hollered from the town/Mess around/And heard Yuk and Knum/Said, 'I gotta be down'/'Cause new styles is going down/Look around you/Tunes from the Lunz/Spreading round and round you/*[Humpty] *Back to get my O on/They let me flow on/The thirty-five on it/Yeah, I'm on it/*[Shock G] *Still bringing satin for them drawers/Velvet for the mic/And got a pound for the cause.*" That verse once again proved that Shock G was more than a caricature and the "I Got 5 on It" remix allowed some of L.A.'s most underrated emcees to shine.

7. "L.A., L.A." [Kuwait Mix] – Capone-N-Noreaga (featuring Mobb Deep & Tragedy Khadafi) (1997)

In 1995, Tha Dogg Pound (comprised of Daz and Kurupt) released their debut album, *Dogg Food*, which included a track featuring Snoop Doggy Dogg called "New York, New York." Although no NYC artists were actually named in the song, the East Coast did not take kindly to the song and Tha Dogg Pound's trailer was even hit with several bullets when the group was in the city to film the song's video. Some East Coast emcees also took offense and decided to return the favor with "**L.A., L.A.**," the video of which portrayed Capone-N-Noreaga and Mobb Deep kidnapping a Kurupt look alike and dropping him off the Queensboro Bridge. Like Prodigy's chorus, the original version of the song mimicked the "New York, New York," beat, but Marley Marl's grittier Kuwait Mix harkened back to the boom bap days of hip-hop's golden age. Most of the rhymes were not-so-subtle threats directed at Tha Dogg Pound and the rest of Death Row's roster, as Tragedy Khadafi stole the show with the song's final verse: *"Been on this planet for 25 years and still strong/The world's rotten like the veins in my father's arm/I remain calm, study Islam, read the Torah/World going in flames like Sodom and Gomorrah/Niggas dried up, laying in the box from the virus/Commercial thugs tried to bust gats at the livest/This life of crime, only will shine real survivors/Y'all half-way niggas, I'd advise you not to try this/So brace yourself, before you get yourself laced/Fucking with the sick Arabic Scarface."* The so-called "East Coast/West Coast" War was quite possibly the worst thing that ever happened in hip-hop, taking the lives of the genre's legends and ripping the culture apart at the seams, but it was the impetus for some terrific music that continues to live on.

6. "Rainy Dayz" [Remix] – Raekwon (featuring Ghostface Killah)

(1995)

Wu-Tang Clan member Raekwon's debut *Only Built 4 Cuban Linx...* was a marked change from the previous releases by the clan and its members, eschewing the hard battle rhymes for a Mafioso storytelling approach that would inspire Nas, Jay-Z, The Notorious B.I.G., and others. Similarly, the remix to "**Rainy Dayz**," one of the strongest cuts on *Cuban Linx...* was vastly different from the original. While the latter was a vintage RZA beat – dark, gloomy, and brooding – Mr. Dalvin's remix presents a much more hopeful sound and both the hook (*"You know how to love me/Makes me feel so good (Let it rain, let it rain)"*) and the lyrics match that mood: *"Due to the wicked, dice should never lie/Now that's a damn lie/proving on standby/Man why?/The game/I mentally tear down the brain/Half of us will feel the pain, big boy/Let it rain/I guess my whole team is marvelous/Street life novelist/Let it rain, dun/Swallow this."* Wu-Tang has never been known for its optimism, but this remix is so buoyant and uplifting that it could have been called "Sunny Dayz."

5. "Paid in Full" [Seven Minutes of Madness – Coldcut Remix] – Eric B. & Rakim (1988)

The only reason a one verse song would be extended to last more than seven minutes is that the beat is transcendent and the "**Paid in Full**" remix fits that description perfectly. Whereas the original cut was basic and stripped down, this version is the complete opposite – complex and multilayered with a shapeshifting beat that never seems repetitive. The incorporation of Israeli singer Ofra Haza's melodic voice from her single "Im Nin'Alu" adds soulfulness, and a variety of vocal samples, especially a woman exclaiming, "You make me feel so good!," bring depth and personality to a track that is about 75% instrumental. Add to that the fact that Rakim's classic verse, written to the original beat, fits the remix like a glove when it begins at the 2:05 mark: *"Thinking of a master plan/'Cause ain't nothing but sweat inside my hand/So I dig into my pocket, all my money is spent/So I dig deeper, but still coming up with lint/So I start my* *mission, leave my residence/Thinking how could I get some dead presidents/I need money, I used to be a stick-up kid/So I think of all the devious things I did/I used to roll up, this is a holdup/Ain't nothing funny/Stop smiling, be still/Don't nothing move but the money.*" Although it was released nearly 25 years ago, the Coldcut Remix's beat is so timeless that it has been used by other artists since its creation, further proving its greatness.

4. "Scenario" [Remix] – A Tribe Called Quest (featuring Leaders of the New School & Kid Hood) (1992)

It's nearly impossible to improve upon one of the greatest posse cuts in history, but A Tribe Called Quest and friends did just that with the remix to their celebrated hit, "**Scenario**." The uptempo beat that drives the original is stripped down to a simple loop with a vocal sample of a voice repeating, "Alright!" that is vintage Tribe and allows the emcees to shine over it. While there are seven vocalists on the track, it was newcomer Kid Hood that stole the show with his opening verse: "*Hood/Madman/I rip up stages/Lay down in your wages, I'm wild like Larry Davis/Extra, extra, pick up a clip. I'll tear ass out the frame/And grab my dick/I'm a Rock'em Sock'em Robot/Kid, I drop bombs/I'm rugged and deadly, so I shit on the petty/I baseball bat a bastard/I'm bad news, I'm crazy and clever/cut does your crews.*" Hood was killed a mere three days after recording his verse, which Busta Rhymes references in the song's introduction: "*Here in 1992, we present the fabulous what's the 'Scenario' remix. Whereas there are seven emcees: six which are in the physical form, one which is in spiritual essence...and he goes by the name of, uh...Hood!*" A Tribe Called Quest is considered one of the greatest groups in history and Busta Rhymes is a legendary solo artist, but for one song they were all overshadowed by a young artist named Kid Hood. He never recorded again, but his legacy lives on in his one verse as part of a hip-hop classic.

3. "Shut 'Em Down" [Pete Rock Remix] – Public Enemy (featuring Pete Rock) (1991)

Pete Rock is a legendary producer known for incorporating horns into his best beats and while Public Enemy usually sounded best over their in-house production team The Bomb Squad's bass-heavy tracks, he made Chuck D sound right at home over those familiar horns on the "**Shut 'Em Down**" remix. The song is so good because Rock managed to merge his own style with that of the Bomb Squad to create a virtually perfect hybrid between the two to play under Chuck D's always strong lyrics: *"I testified/My mama cried/Black people died/When the other man lied/See the TV, listen to me/Double trouble/I overhaul and I'm coming from the lower level/I'm taking tabs/Sho' 'nuff/Stuff to grab/Like shirts and it hurts/With a neck to wreck/Took a poll/'Cause our soul/Took a toll/From the education/Of a TV station/But look around/Hear go the sound/Of the wrecking ball/Boom and pound/When I shut 'em down."* Pete Rock also contributed a verse of his own, but it is his beat that ultimately takes this remix to the next level.

2. "Flava In Ya Ear" [Remix] – Craig Mack (feat. The Notorious B.I.G., Rampage, LL Cool J & Busta Rhymes) (1994)

In 1994, Sean Combs decided to build his fledgling record label, Bad Boy Records, around two artists – Craig Mack and The Notorious B.I.G. – and promoted them with fast food sandwich boxes that said "B.I.G. Mack" on them. However, the two only recorded together one song, the "**Flava In Ya Ear**" remix, which resulted in both a top five posse cut and a top five remix. Mack and B.I.G. were joined by LL Cool J, Rampage, and Busta Rhymes (as well as some quintessential Puff Daddy adlibs) over Easy Mo Bee's infectious, head banging beat. Every emcee had lines that forced the listener to press rewind, but it was Biggie's verse to kick off the song that resonated the most: *"Niggas is mad, I get more butt than ashtrays/Fuck a fair one, I get mines the fast way/The ski mask way/Uhh/Ransom notes/Far from handsome, but damn a nigga* *tote/(What ya' tote?)/More guns than roses/Foes is/Shaking in their boots/Invisible bullies like The Gooch/Disappear/Vamoose/You're wack to me/Take them rhymes back to the factory/I see/The gimmicks/The wack lyrics/The shit is depressing/Pathetic/Please forget it/You're mad 'cause my style you're admiring/Don't be mad, UPS is hiring/You should've been a cop/Fuck hip-hop/With that freestyle, you're bound to get shot/Not from Houston, but I **Rap-A-Lot**/Pack the gat a lot/The flav's 'bout to drop/Uhh."* Considering how great this remix turned out, hip-hop would have benefited from a few more Craig Mack and The Notorious B.I.G. collaborations.

1. "One More Chance/Stay with Me" [Remix] – The Notorious B.I.G. (featuring Faith Evans & Mary J. Blige) (1995)

It was already clear that he had unlimited potential, but The Notorious B.I.G. became a hip-hop superstar upon the release of his third single, the remix to his song "**One More Chance**." The original was an album cut with a rugged, thumping bass line over which B.I.G. kicks explicit rhymes about his bedroom proficiency. The remix offered an entirely different vibe that sounded like an R&B song and featured a laidback Biggie being a bit more romantic over a beat of rolling piano keys sampled from the Debarge song "Stay with Me" and Faith Evans serenading him on the chorus (with Mary J. Blige providing additional vocals). He may not have looked the part of a sex symbol, but B.I.G. was a ladies man for the way he put words together: *"The finest women, I love with a passion/Your man's a wimp, I give that ass a good thrashing/High fashion/Flying into all states/Sexing me while your man masturbates/Isn't this great?/Your flight leaves at eight/Her flight lands at nine, my game just rewind/Lyrically I'm supposed to represent/I'm not only the client, I'm the player president."* Sean "Puffy" Combs claims that he and his Bad Boy cohorts invented the concept of the remix and "One More Chance" is the pinnacle of that concept.

Honorable Mentions

"187 um" ["Deep Cover" Remix] – Dr. Dre (featuring Snoop Doggy Dogg) (1992)

"Ebonics" [DJ Premier Remix] – Big L (1998)

"I Got Cha Opin" [Remix] – Black Moon (1994)

THE HIP-HOP 10

Interlude

I am not a musician.

While I have been listening to, and even amateurishly researching, hip-hop for more than twenty years, I can't work turntables or create a beat or even play any instrument at all. I don't really know the difference between a kick, a snare, and a hi-hat. When I hear music, I can tell you if I like it or not, but I can't really tell you the specifics of why. I'm sure you've noticed that this book focuses on lyrics more than beats. There are two reasons for this. First, it is much easier to convey the power of lyrics via the written word. When an artist's verse is presented on a page, a reader will immediately hear that artist's voice reciting those lyrics in his or her head. That process becomes much more difficult when trying to use words to accurately describe how something sounds. Secondly, I know far more about lyrics than I do about beats. I can deconstruct rhymes from a variety of ways, but the only way I can analyze the music is by trying to describe the sounds using basic terminology that only emphasizes my ignorance in creating music.

As a result, you'll notice that the next chapter is different from all of the others in that it is only a listing of my choices of the best hip-hop beats in history without any narrative supporting or explaining my rankings. It is only temporary – all of the following chapters will be in the same format as those in the first half of this book.

Let's return to our regularly scheduled program…

THE HIP-HOP 10

5. THE BEST BEATS OF ALL TIME

10. "Whoa!" – Black Rob (2000)

9. "Straight Outta Compton" – N.W.A (1988)

8. "Shook Ones (Part II)" – Mobb Deep (1995)

7. "Criminology" – Raekwon f/ Ghostface Killah (1995)

6. "N.Y. State of Mind" – Nas (1994)

5. "Still D.R.E." – Dr. Dre f/ Snoop Dogg (1999)

4. "All About The Benjamins" – Puff Daddy f/ The LOX, Lil' Kim & The Notorious B.I.G. (1997)

3. "Reunited" – Wu-Tang Clan (1997)

2. "The Symphony" – Juice Crew (1988)

1. "Who Shot Ya?" – The Notorious B.I.G. (1995)

Honorable Mentions

"Triumph" – Wu-Tang Clan (1997)

"Deep Cover" – Dr. Dre f/ Snoop Doggy Dogg (1992)

"Flava in Ya Ear" – Craig Mack (1994)

"Get Ur Freak On" – Missy Elliot (2001)

"Lucifer" – Jay-Z (2003)

"You Know My Steez" – Gang Starr (1998)

4. THE BEST HIP-HOP ALBUMS OF ALL TIME

10. *Reasonable Doubt* (1996) – Jay-Z

Although he had been featured on tracks by heavyweights such as Big Daddy Kane, Big L and his mentor, The Jaz, Jay-Z was rejected by every major record label and decided to release his debut album independently. The result, **Reasonable Doubt**, launched both Roc-A-Fella Records and one of the most successful solo careers in music history. While he had made a name for himself in the underground with his method speed rapping, Jay eased up on the gas pedal and in the process added much more complexity to his lyrics. It was originally meant to be the *only* Jay-Z album, so *Reasonable Doubt* is the culmination of twenty-six years of a clever wordsmith that repeatedly chose crime over rhyme. On the surface, the subject matter seemed to be similar to what many artists were doing, but what made *Reasonable Doubt* different from the other albums of the era was that Jay-Z was explaining – and trying to reconcile – the pain that Sean Carter had inflicted on his people and his neighborhood. As opposed to so many albums before (and after) it, Jay's debut was not just a glorification of the so-called "gangster" lifestyle, but rather an explanation of it, with the hindsight and voice of experience. The LP, ranked the 248th greatest album of all time by *Rolling Stone*, is loaded with classic songs, from the smoothness of "Can't Knock the Hustle," to the boasting duet with The Notorious B.I.G., "Brooklyn's Finest," to the celebratory, "Can I Live," but the closing track, "Regrets," gives the listener a window into the mind of an introspective hustler that realizes the Faustian bargain that he made: *"As sure as this/Earth is turning souls burning/In search of higher learning/Turning in every direction/Seeking direction/My mom's crying/'Cause her insides are dying/Her son trying her patience/Keep her heart racing/A million beats a minute/I know I push you to your limit/But it's this game, love/I'm caught up all in it/They make it so you can't prevent it/Never give it, you got to take it/Can't fake it/I keep it authentic."* Before he was a global icon gracing the cover of *Forbes* alongside Warren Buffett, Jay-Z was just a young artist that wanted to tell his story. That story turned out to be a classic.

9. *Only Built 4 Cuban Linx…* (1995) – Raekwon

Between 1994 and 1996, five of the Wu-Tang Clan's nine members released solo albums. All were critically acclaimed and commercially successful, but the third release was not only the best of the five, it was one of the best solo debut albums in the history of hip-hop. **Only Built 4 Cuban Linx…** was loosely presented as a feature film that follows two criminals as they try to perform one last job before leaving behind the life of crime, with Raekwon as the star, Ghostface Killah as the guest star, and RZA as the director, with guest appearances by every Wu-Tang member. Often referred to as "The Purple Tape" because of the color of the cassette's plastic to differentiate it just as drug dealers do with their product, the LP marked a change of direction for the Clan, featuring slower beats reminiscent of crime films and Rae's lyrics followed suit, revolving around mafia-like story rhymes as opposed to his rapid-fire battle approach he featured on "Meth vs. Chef" from Method Man's solo album. Every Wu member adopted a mafia alias for the project (Raekwon as Lou Diamond, Ghostface as Tony Starks, Method Man as Johnny Blaze, etc…) and five of the members came together to explore this theme on the influential "Wu-Gambinos." The disc is almost perfectly balanced, contrasting criminally-oriented tracks such as "Criminology," "Rainy Dayz," and "Ice Water" with the introspective "Can It Be All So Simple"

[Remix] and the radio-friendly ode to females of every race, "Ice Cream." The album's standout track, "Verbal Intercourse," marked the first time a non-Clan-affiliated member appeared on a Wu-Tang effort as Nas performed one of the most memorable verses of all time: *"Through the lights, cameras and action, glamour, glitters and gold/I unfold the scroll, plant seeds to stampede the globe/When I'm deceased, by then the beast will rise like yeast/To conquer peace, Leaving savages to roam in the streets/Live on the run, police paying me to give in my gun/Trick my wisdom with the system that imprisoned my son/Smoke a gold leaf, I hold heat, nonchalantly/I'm raunchy, the things I do is real and never haunts me/While funny style niggas roll in the pile/Rooster heads profile on a bus to Riker's Isle/Holding weed inside they pussy with they minds on the pretty things in life/Props is a true thug's wife/It's like a cycle, niggas come home, some will go in/Do a bullet, come back, do the same shit again/From the womb to the tomb/Presume the unpredictable/Guns salute life, rapidly, that's the ritual."* The impact of *Only Built 4 Cuban Linx…* was immediate, as Raekwon set the standard of mid-'90s East Coast hip-hop with mob-themed lyrics from felonious alter egos, a practice that was copied on by Nas (as Nas Escobar) on *It Was Written*, The Notorious B.I.G. (as Frank White) on *Life After Death*, and even 2Pac (as Makaveli) on *All Eyez On Me*. When three of the greatest emcees in history copy a style, it's clearly influential.

8. *Paul's Boutique* (1989) – Beastie Boys

Over the course of their nearly thirty year career, the Beastie Boys released eight studio albums to both critical and commercial success. **Paul's Boutique**, the group's second LP, was not the most commercially successful, but it is undoubtedly the most significant – to the entire music industry. In an effort to distance themselves from their juvenile (yet extremely successful) debut on their now-former label, Def Jam, the group was intent on making a more creative and layered album the second time around. As a result, the Beasties, along with the innovative production duo the Dust Brothers, emerged from the studio with a groundbreaking album that was originally viewed as a disappointment but, over time, became a landmark LP in the annals of hip-hop history. Originally conceived as a Dust Brothers instrumental album, the beats on the album were much more dense and complex than the music found on other hip-hop albums since they were made to stand on their own without any vocal accompaniment. The fifteen track album sampled 105 songs, a feat that was only possible before Gilbert O'Sullivan won his 1991 lawsuit against Biz Markie that greatly increased the costs of sampling music going forward. That is half of what makes *Paul's Boutique,* ranked as the 156th greatest album of all time by *Rolling Stone*, so significant – it will never be duplicated. The other half is the classic Beastie wit and wordplay, featured on classic tracks like "Hey Ladies," "Johnny Ryall," the nine-part finale, "B-Boy Bouillabaisse," and best evidenced on "Shake Your Rump": *"Like Sam the butcher bringing Alice the meat/Like Fred Flintstone driving around with bald feet/Should I have another sip? No, skip it/In the back of the ride and bust with the whippet/Rope a dope dookies all around the neck/Woo ha!/Got them all in check/Running from the law, the press, and the parents/(Is your name Michael Diamond?)/No, mine's Clarence/From downtown Manhattan/The village/My style is wild and you know that it still is/Disco bag schlepping and you're doing the bump/Shake your rump."* Although *Licensed to Ill* sold more records, there is no doubt as to what is the group's greatest work. A watershed moment in American music, there will never be another album as creative or multifaceted as *Paul's Boutique*.

7. *Enter the Wu-Tang [36 Chambers]* (1993) – Wu-Tang Clan

Although no one knew it at the time, an unknown group of nine emcees from an overlooked New York borough created a streetwise debut album full of chess and kung fu references that not only signaled the beginning of that group's five-year reign, but also influenced an entire generation of rappers and producers. When the Staten Island-based group Wu-Tang Clan's debut, **Enter the Wu-Tang [36 Chambers]**, was released it was so original and different from everything else at the time that no one really knew how to respond to it. The production was gritty, static could be heard on the samples, and sound effects were used to bleep out profanities. The album sounded like a demo that had been recorded in RZA's basement (which, in fact, it had) and was the complete opposite of Dr. Dre's perfectly polished West Coast sound. *36 Chambers* was like nothing most fans had ever heard and, as a result, it took time for it to ingratiate itself in the genre, never placing higher than 41st on the *Billboard* chart. Perhaps that only enhanced its legacy. Wu-Tang wrested control of listeners' ears from Death Row and, in the process, opened the gates for the great New York debuts that would follow, such as *Illmatic, Ready to Die, The Infamous, Reasonable Doubt*, and others. "Protect Ya Neck," "Can It Be All So Simple," and "Method Man," all stand the test of time, but the album's second single, "C.R.E.A.M.," propelled the group into the spotlight, introduced a new synonym for money, and was listed by *Time* as one of the all-time 100 greatest songs. With standout verses from both Raekwon and Inspectah Deck, it was Method Man's catchy hook that made the song so popular: *"Cash rules everything around me/C.R.E.A.M./Get the money/Dollar dollar bill, y'all!"* Listed at 386 on *Rolling Stone*'s top 500 album list, *Enter the Wu-Tang [36 Chambers]*, made stars out of several group members, most notably Ol' Dirty Bastard and Method Man, and also laid the foundation for the five Wu-Tang solo albums that would be sandwiched between it and the group's follow-up, *Wu-Tang Forever*. It also marked the beginning of RZA's five-year plan, in which he asked that the rest of the group members wholly defer to him and, in exchange, he would make them the biggest hip-hop act in the world within five years. It was a promise he kept and it all started with *36 Chambers*.

6. *Ready to Die* (1994) – The Notorious B.I.G.

After hearing the demo tape of a rapper named Biggie Smalls, Sean "Puffy" Combs immediately signed him to Uptown Records, where he was employed. Soon thereafter, Combs was fired from Uptown and it appeared that Smalls' music career was over before it ever really began. Combs, however, did not give up and, a year later, both a superstar and a classic were born. The Notorious B.I.G.'s **Ready to Die** was the first album on Combs' new imprint, Bad Boy Records, and although it was released five months after Nas's seminal *Illmatic*, it was far more popular, with several songs receiving heavy airplay and turning fans' attention away from Los Angeles and back to New York City. Ranked as the 133rd greatest album of all time by *Rolling Stone*, *Ready to Die* is the ultimate concept album – the album opens with a crying newborn, is filled with sound effects and scripted dialogue, and ends with the sound of a self-inflicted gunshot wound after the final song, "Suicidal Thoughts." In between, B.I.G. takes us through the highs and lows of his world in Brooklyn, from the celebratory "Juicy" and the arrogant "Big Poppa," to the violent "Gimme the Loot" and the desperate "Everyday Struggle." It is on this track that the cocky veneer of a hardcore rapper is replaced by a distressed expectant father worrying about how to survive on a day-to-day basis while still employing double- and triple-internal rhyme schemes and clever wordplay: *"I know how it feel to wake up fucked up/Pockets broke as hell, another rock to sell/People look at you like you's the user/Selling drugs to all the losers, mad buddha abuser/But they don't know about your stress-filled day/Baby on the way, mad bills to pay/That's why you drink Tanqueray, so you can reminisce/And wish, you wasn't living so devilish, shit/I remember I was just like you/Smoking blunts with my crew, flipping over 62's/'Cause G-E-D wasn't B-I-G/I got P-A-I-D, that's why my mom's hate me/She was forced to kick me out, no doubt/Then I figured out nicks went for twenty down South/Packed up my tools for my raw power move/Glock nineteen for casket and flower moves/For chumps trying to stop my flow/And what they don't know will show on the autopsy/Went to see Papi, to cop me a brick/Asked for some consignment and he wasn't trying to hear it/Smoking mad Newports/'Cause I'm due in court/For an assault that I caught/In Bridgeport, New York/Catch me if you can like the Gingerbread Man/You better have your gat in hand, cause man...* [Chorus] *I don't wanna live no more/Sometimes I hear death knocking at my front door/I'm living everyday like a hustle, another drug to juggle/Another day, another* *struggle."* The greatest strength of *Ready to Die* is that every feeling, good and bad, is touched on, expressed, explored, and appraised. The album includes a song that speaks to virtually every emotion and that is why it continues to resonate nearly twenty years later.

5. *Straight Outta Compton* (1988) – N.W.A

"You are now about to witness the strength of street knowledge." That is how Dr. Dre introduced N.W.A's debut album and it's quite possible that truer words have never been spoken on record. It's difficult to name an album released in the past 30 years that has had more of a cultural impact than **Straight Outta Compton**. In addition to establishing California as a legitimate hotbed for heavyweight emcees, that one LP, which landed at 144th on *Rolling Stone*'s list of the 500 Greatest Albums of All Time, put the grim reality of living in South Central Los Angeles into the national spotlight and birthed the subgenre of "gangster rap" in the process. Although its members were all unknown at the time, N.W.A was a supergroup that made the world realize that the West Coast was more than just sunshine, palm trees, and Hollywood. Dr. Dre & DJ Yella's hard-pounding, pulsating beats created a frenzied backdrop over which Ice Cube, MC Ren, and group leader Eazy-E delivered the most violent and vivid lyrics ever heard in hip-hop at the time, giving the quintet the title of "the world's most dangerous group." The album was packed with future classics, from the title track to the crossover hit, "Express Yourself," to the storytelling cuts, "Gangsta, Gangsta," and "Dopeman" [Remix], to the highly controversial, "Fuck tha Police," which included lyrics so inflammatory that it led to a joint investigation by the FBI and Secret Service. Ice Cube: *"Fuck tha police/Coming straight from the underground/A young nigga got it bad 'cause I'm brown/And not the other color so police think/They have the authority to kill a minority/Fuck that shit, 'cause I ain't the one/For a punk motherfucker with a badge and a gun/To be beating on/And thrown in jail/We could go toe to toe in the middle of a cell/Fucking with me 'cause I'm a teenager/With a little bit of gold and a pager/Searching my car, looking for the product/Thinking every*

nigga is selling narcotics." The collective would not last long but the success and influence of every member can be directly attributed to *Straight Outta Compton*.

4. *Paid in Full* (1987) – Eric B. & Rakim

When Eric B. & Rakim's **Paid in Full** was released in the summer of 1987, it introduced a new era in how rap artists wrote and presented their rhymes. While Eric B.'s production was impressive, particularly in its use of stacking samples, it was Rakim's lyrics that elevated the disc to classic status and forever changed the style of hip-hop. At the time, hip-hop was loud, with artists sounding like Run-DMC, often yelling their basic lyrics and call-and-response rhymes over thunderous beats that created a kind of urban rock sound. In contrast, Rakim treated the music as an artform, calmly speaking to the listener while simultaneously informing everyone that he was not one that you should take lightly ("*I take this more serious than just a poem*"). By introducing internal rhyme schemes and referencing far deeper and more complex content than other artists at the time without ever raising his voice, Rakim created the foundation for the future of hip-hop. Coming in at 227 on *Rolling Stone*'s top 500 albums and containing multiple unforgettable cuts including "I Ain't No Joke," "My Melody," and "I Know You Got Soul," *Paid in Full* became more than just an LP – it became an audio manual for a generation of artists that wanted to learn how to become the best. Every great emcee that came after, from Jay-Z to Eminem to Nas and everyone in between, readily acknowledges that both Rakim and *Paid in Full* were heavy influences in the development of their careers and their styles. Rakim was so far ahead of everyone else that it almost seemed like he was from another time and place. The first time most people heard this prophet of lyricism was on the duo's debut single, "Eric B. is President," and Ra's first verse has often been called the greatest verse in hip-hop history and has been borrowed, quoted, and sampled countless times: "*I came in the door, I said it before/I never let the mic magnetize me no more/But it's biting me, fighting me, inviting me to rhyme/I can't hold it back, I'm looking for the* line/Taking off my coat, clearing my throat/My rhyme will be kicking it until I hit my last note/My mind'll range to find all kinds of ideas/Self-esteem makes it seem like a thought took years to build/But still say a rhyme after the next one/Prepared, never scared, I'll just bless one/And you know that I'm the soloist/So Eric B., make 'em clap to this..." Without *Paid in Full*, it's possible that hip-hop would have never evolved from its rudimentary roots or, if it had, it would have happened far later than 1987.

3. *The Chronic* (1992) – Dr. Dre

After Dr. Dre left N.W.A and Ruthless Records, many believed that his career was over. Instead, he co-founded Death Row Records, recruited a roster of talented up-and-coming artists, and once again changed the sound and direction of hip-hop with his debut solo LP, **The Chronic**. He called his new sound, a mixture of Parliament-Funkadelic samples, soulful hooks, live instrumentation, and trunk-rattling beats, "G-Funk." Initially, Dre only wanted to supply the beats, leaving the raps to Death Row's roster of young spitters, all of whom were hungry to prove themselves. Although he was eventually convinced to lend his own vocals to the project, Dre still gave a platform to his new labelmates, the collective of which would become known as the "Death Row Inmates," a murderer's row of soon-to-be household names: RBX, The Lady of Rage, Nate Dogg, the duo of Daz and Kurupt known as Tha Dogg Pound, and future superstar Snoop Doggy Dogg. While the album made Snoop an overnight sensation, he was not the only one that made the most of the opportunity, evidenced by Kurupt's jaw-dropping verse that led "Stranded on Death Row": "*Stranded on Death Row, so duck when I swing my shit/I get rugged like Rawhead Rex with fat tracks that fits/The gangsta type, what I recite's kind-of lethal/Niggas know, The flow that I kick, there's no refill/I'm murdering niggas, yo, and maybe because of the tone I kicks/When I grip the mic and kick shit/Niggas can't fuck with/So remember I go hardcore, and slam/'Nuff respect like a sensei, whoop ass like Van Damme/So any nigga that claim they're bossin'/What don't you* bring your ass on over to Crenshaw and Slauson?/Take a walk through the hood, where we up to no good/Slanging on things like a real O./G should, I'm stacking and macking and packing a grip and/When you're slippin', I slip the clip in/But ain't no set tripppin'/'Cause it's Death Row rolling like the mafia/Thinking about whooping some ass, but what the fuck's stopping ya?/Ain't nathan but a buster/I'm stranded on Death Row for pumping slugs in motherfuckers/Now you know you're outdone/Feel the shotgun/Kurupt inmate, cell block one."* Such rugged and raw lyrics over Dre's funky beats made *The Chronic*, ranked 137th on *Rolling Stone*'s list of the 500 greatest albums of all time, the blueprint for every West Coast album for the next decade – until he would do it again seven years later with his follow-up, *2001*.

2. *Illmatic* (1994) – Nas

In 1994, hip-hop was living in the post-*Chronic* era and while Wu-Tang Clan had brought attention back to New York, the birthplace of hip-hop was still searching for a new messiah with introspective and thought-provoking lyrics to lead the East Coast into a new age. Enter 21 year-old Nasir Jones. Following a few scene-stealing guest appearances and a song ("Halftime") on the soundtrack to the film *Zebrahead*, expectations for the young emcee's first album were sky high. Somehow he exceeded those expectations. While *Straight Outta Compton* could be likened to the evening nightly news with N.W.A informing the public of what was happening in their neighborhood, **Illmatic** was more like a documentary as Nas brought his listeners into Queensbridge and not only expressed the things he witnessed, but also tried to make sense of it all. Stylistically, *Illmatic* boasted a collection of sparse and harsh beats that were each unique, a result of it being one of the first albums to feature a variety of producers rather than just a single beat maker or team. Behind the microphone, Nas's contemplative lyrics, poetic flow, and calm delivery drew favorable comparisons to Rakim as both created new standards for lyrical ability on their respective debuts. With Nas rhyming over classic beats from the likes of DJ Premier, Large Professor, L.E.S., Q-Tip, and Pete

Rock, *Illmatic* was the prototype for mid-'90s East Coast hip-hop, landing at 400 on *Rolling Stone*'s greatest albums list. After the introduction, the first actual song on the LP is "N.Y. State of Mind," an epic tale of life on the street with a Premier beat that immediately grabs the listener's attention and allows Nas to gain the admiration of the entire genre: "*So now I'm jetting to the building lobby/And it was filled with children probably couldn't see as high as I be/(So what you saying?)/ It's like the game ain't the same/Got younger niggas pulling the triggers, bringing fame to their name/And claim some corners, crews without guns are goners/In broad daylight, stickup kids – they run up on us/45's and gauges, Macs, in fact/Same niggas will catch a back-to-back, snatching your cracks in black/There was a snitch on the block getting niggas knocked/So hold your stash 'til the coke price drop/I know this crackhead who said she's got to smoke nice rock/And if it's good, she'll bring you customers in measuring pots/But yo/You gotta slide on a vacation, inside information/Keeps large niggas erasing and their wives basing/It drops deep as it does in my breath/I never sleep, 'cause sleep is the cousin of death/Beyond the walls of intelligence, life is defined/I think of crime when I'm in a New York state of mind*." That one song set the entire tone for the resurgence of lyrics-driven East Coast hip-hop over the next several years. The album's vibe continues to vacillate emotionally, from the honest "Life's A Bitch" (featuring a career-making verse from AZ), to the bravado of "Represent," to the letter to an incarcerated friend on "One Love," all of which combine to paint a vivid and detailed picture of a young man that has seen far too much pain and suffering in his own life but refuses to give in. Towards the end of "N.Y. State of Mind," Nas proclaims, "*Life is parallel to Hell but I must maintain*," a sentence that could sum up the entirety of not only *Illmatic*, but also a generation of young people that saw it as a soundtrack to their lives.

1. *It Takes a Nation of Millions to Hold Us Back* (1988) – Public Enemy

When the time came to being recording their second album, Public Enemy decided that they would eschew the carefree, party-heavy approach that most artists used in the late '80s and instead create an album full of social commentary. The result is a masterpiece. Ranked by *Rolling Stone* as the 48th greatest album in history, **It Takes a Nation of Millions to Hold Us Back** is the highest hip-hop entry on the list by a wide margin (the second-highest is all the way down at 122). Deservedly so. The album is loud, fast, dense, multilayered, deep, honest, and raw. The Bomb Squad used multiple samples – as many as twenty in a single track – to build a musical bed over which Chuck D spoke truth to power and promoted pro-black Afrocentrism while Flavor Flav showed that the group still had a sense of humor. It has become the standard for rappers to boast about their (sometimes fictitious) life of crime, but Public Enemy took the opposite approach by railing against what crack cocaine had done to inner-cities by likening addicts to zombies on "Night of the Living Baseheads." Additionally, the album criticized the media ("Don't Believe the Hype"), music industry exploitation ("Caught, Can We Get a Witness?"), promoted the freedom to protest ("Party for Your Right to Fight") and detailed a prison break ("Black Steel in the Hour of Chaos"). In response to the criticism that hip-hop was just noise and not actually music, the group made "Bring the Noise," to show that they would not be deterred: "*Never badder than bad cause the brother is madder than mad/At the fact that's corrupt as a senator/Soul on a roll, but you treat it like soap on a rope/'Cause the beats and the lines are so dope/Listen for lessons I'm saying inside music that the critics are blasting me for/They'll never care for the brothers and sisters now, cause the country has us up for the war/We got to demonstrate, come on now/They're gonna have to wait/'Til we get it right/Radio stations I question their blackness/They call themselves black, but we'll see if they'll play this.*" P.E. brought self-awareness and consciousness to a culture that was sorely lacking both at the time and while many things have changed in the quarter-decade since the release of *It Takes a Nation of Millions to Hold Us Back*, many things haven't and much of what is addressed on the album could very well be describing today's world. The timelessness is just one of the many reasons that make it the great hip-hop album of all time.

Honorable Mentions

Midnight Marauders – A Tribe Called Quest

The Blueprint – Jay-Z

Things Fall Apart – The Roots

Resurrection – Common Sense

3. THE BEST PRODUCERS OF ALL TIME

10. The Bomb Squad

For about a five year span, Public Enemy was the most ferocious musical act in the country and although Chuck D's vocals certainly contributed, much of the group's power came from the angry, nonstop beats that **The Bomb Squad** created. Consisting of Hank and Keith Shocklee, Eric "Vietnam" Salder, Gary G-Wiz, Kerwin "Sleek" Young, and Chuck D himself, the production team was the driving force behind much of P.E.'s early work. While the team became best known for its bombastic, dense, heavily sampled beats, its sounds were more eclectic than most people realize. While Public Enemy's 1988 classic *It Takes a Nation of Millions to Hold Us Back* featured the quintessential Bomb Squad sound, the follow-up, 1990's *Fear of a Black Planet*, showcased beats that were far more complex and a bit more experimental. It was between those two albums that respect for the team reached another level when a young emcee traveled 3,000 miles for the opportunity to work with them. When Ice Cube left N.W.A, very few people believed he would be able to make it as a solo artist, particularly since he would no longer have Dr. Dre making his beats. In a bold move for the time, Cube relocated to New York City and tapped Shocklee and company to provide his solo debut with the same viciousness they had for Public Enemy. The outcome was *AmeriKKKa's Most Wanted*, a bicoastal classic that proved Ice Cube could survive without N.W.A. and the team could survive without Public Enemy. And

P.E. and Cube weren't the only beneficiaries of the Bomb Squad treatment. Such varied acts as 3rd Bass ("Steppin' to the A.M."), Slick Rick ("Teenage Love"), LL Cool J ("It Gets No Rougher"), Run-DMC ("Ooh, Whatcha Gonna Do"), Bell Biv Devoe ("Ain't Nut'in' Changed"), and Young Black Teenagers ("Loud & Hard To Hit") all featured the Bomb Squad sound in the late '80s and early '90s. Although the team is ostensibly retired, its contribution to hip-hop, both in its methods and its products, cannot be overlooked.

9. The Neptunes

Commercial success is often a double-edge sword, as wealth and fame often comes at the expense of artistic integrity. The production duo of Chad Hugo and Pharrell Williams, known as **The Neptunes**, don't seem to suffer from that problem, probably because they've been creating chart-topping hits their entire careers, with twenty-four (and counting) songs that charted in the *Billboard* Hot 100 top ten. The pair won a Grammy in 2004 for Producer of the Year and were named Producer(s) of the Decade at the *Billboard* R&B/Hip-Hop Awards. A couple of self-proclaimed nerds (hence their group name of N.E.R.D.), Hugo and Williams use a variety of sounds and instruments (including classical instruments like a cello and a tuba as well as mouth clicks and pops) that had never before been considered in hip-hop. Their hit list is long and varied, featuring the genre's biggest acts of the past fifteen years: Mase ("Lookin' At Me"), Noreaga ("Superthug [What What]," "Oh No," "Nothin'"), Kelis ("Caught Out There"), Ol' Dirty Bastard ("Got Your Money"), Jay-Z ("I Just Wanna Love U [Give It To Me]," "Excuse Me Miss," "Change Clothes"), Ludacris ("Southern Hospitality," "Money Maker"), Busta Rhymes & P. Diddy ("Pass The Courvoisier Part II"), Fabolous ("Holla Back [Young'n]"), Jadakiss ("Knock Yourself Out"), Philly's Most Wanted ("Cross The Border"), LL Cool J ("Luv U Better"), Nas ("The Flyest"), Snoop Dogg ("Beautiful," "Drop It Like It's Hot"), Slim Thug ("I Ain't Heard Of That"), Clipse ("Grindin'," "When The Last Time," "Mr. Me Too"), and countless more. The duo has branched out, producing hits in other genres and scoring feature films, but they still come back to what they do best and the list of repeat collaborators prove just how highly regarded they are. While enlisting The Neptunes almost guarantees a hit song, it does so without compromising any artistic integrity or respect, and that is just as impressive as their list of hits.

8. Timbaland

The best word to describe a **Timbaland** beat would be 'futuristic.' Ever since introducing his unorthodox sound on Ginuwine's "Pony," Timothy Mosley has been flooding hip-hop with beats that sound like they're from a galaxy far, far away and has changed the sound of the entire music industry in the process. A 13-time Grammy Award nominee (and two-time winner), he became known thanks to his production of childhood friend Missy Elliot's debut, *Supa Dupa Fly*. The music on that album was both legendary and revolutionary, proving that hip-hop could be more than boom bap drums or disco-era samples. In addition to seven albums of his own (four as a solo artist, three with partner Magoo) and his work producing all or part of Missy's six studio albums, Timbaland was a go-to producer for every big name in the game: Nas ("You Owe Me"), Eminem ("Tylenol Island"), Redman ("Put It Down"), The LOX ("Ryde or Die, Bitch"), Snoop Dogg ("Snoop Dogg [What's My Name Pt. 2]"), Lil' Kim ("The Jump Off"), Ludacris ("Rollout [My Business]"), Fabolous ("Make Me Better"), 50 Cent ("Ayo Technology"), T.I. ("Here We Go Again"), Drake ("Thank Me Now"), The Game ("Put You On The Game"), and, most notably, Jay-Z ("Nigga What, Nigga Who [Originator '99]," "Big Pimpin'," "Hey Papi," "Dirt Off Your Shoulder"). Recently, Timbaland has challenged himself by turning his attention to other genres and has even hinted that he no longer wants to produce hip-hop albums. While that would certainly be a disappointment to listeners everywhere, Timbaland saw the future long before the rest of us and has left an indelible mark on the culture as a result.

7. Rick Rubin

Aside from a few notable exceptions, **Rick Rubin** stopped producing hip-hop music in 1990. The fact that he has been away from the genre for more than two decades and is still one of the ten best producers in history illustrates just how important and influential he was for the growth of the music. A co-founder of Def Jam Recordings, Rubin combined elements of rap and rock long before it was called a mashup, creating the sounds that would solidify hip-hop as a viable form of music rather than simply a passing fad. Rubin was the architect of the early Def Jam sound, producing the debut albums for both the Beastie Boys (*License to Ill*) and LL Cool J (*Radio*), the hits "Christmas in Hollis" by Run-DMC and "Going Back to Cali" by LL, contributing beats for Run-DMC's *Raising Hell* and *Tougher Than Leather*, and executive producing Public Enemy's first two efforts (*Yo! Bum Rush the Show* and *It Takes a Nation of Millions to Hold Us Back*). After leaving Def Jam, Rubin served as executive producer for The Geto Boys and Sir Mix-a-Lot, but spent much of the next couple decades working with rock and alternative artists. However, Rubin proved that he never lost his knack for creating epic beats for emcees with the hard-charging "99 Problems" for Jay-Z in 2003 and the anthemic collaboration "Classic [Better Than I've Ever Been]" for Kanye West, KRS-One, and Nas. Modern-day hip-hop may no longer have the Rick Rubin sound, but, ironically, Rick Rubin's sound was instrumental in creating what we now know as modern-day hip-hop.

6. Marley Marl

The defining sound of East Coast hip-hop for more than a decade was invented – and perfected – by **Marley Marl**. The founder of the legendary Juice Crew, rap's first supergroup that featured legendary artists MC Shan, Big Daddy Kane, Kool G. Rap, Masta Ace, Craig G., and more, Marl was a pioneer of the art of sampling, a practice that resulted in less electronic sounds in favor of grittier-sounding drums and rhythms. The Marley Marl sound was responsible for some of the biggest efforts of the decade, including his own debut album, *In Control, Volume 1*, which featured the legendary posse cut "The Symphony," the MC Shan contributions to the "Bridge Wars" (hip-hop's first major beef), and even resurrecting the slumping career of LL Cool J in 1990. Many classic albums of the late '80s were overseen by Marl: MC Shan (*Down by Law, Born to Be Wild*), Big Daddy Kane (*Long Live the Kane, It's a Big Daddy Thing*), Kool G. Rap (*Road to the Riches, Wanted: Dead or Alive*), LL Cool J (*Mama Said Knock You Out*), Monie Love (*In a Word or 2*), Masta Ace (*Take a Look Around*), and Biz Markie (*Goin' Off*). Furthermore, Marl produced classic songs such as Eric B. & Rakim's "Eric B. Is President," Capone-N-Noreaga's "L.A., L.A. [Kuwait Mix]," Nas's "On the Real," and Raekwon's "Pyrex Vision." Even if Marley Marl never makes another beat, his sound will continue to live on by the legendary producers that were influenced by his work, most notably Pete Rock, DJ Premier, and RZA.

5. Pete Rock

If producers were to be defined by one sound or instrument, there is no doubt that the horn would be the choice for **Pete Rock**. Following in Marley Marl's footsteps with his use of sampling, the "Chocolate Boy Wonder" went in a different direction. In contrast to Marl's more basic beds that featured hard-hitting drums and little else, Rock's beats were much more intricate, with obscure soul and jazz samples being stacked on top of one another to create a virtual orchestra out of a single machine that gave his music a much more mellow vibe. This unique sound was brought to the attention of many through his work as one-half of the duo Pete Rock & C.L. Smooth, who released an EP (*All Souled Out*) and two LP's (*Mecca and the Soul Brother* and *The Main Ingredient*) together. The two's biggest hit, "They Reminisce Over You [T.R.O.Y.]," was a dedication to a deceased friend and Rock's use of a saxophone sample captured the spirit of the song just as well as C.L. Smooth's lyrics. After the two disbanded, Rock went on to produce his own albums – *Soul Survivor, PeteStrumentals, Soul Survivor II*, and *NY's Finest* – as well as numerous songs for legendary artists such as Big L ("Holdin' It Down"), AZ ("Gimme

Yours," "Rather Unique"), Redman ("How to Roll a Blunt"), The Lost Boyz ("The Yearn"), Ghostface Killah & Raekwon ("R.A.G.U."), Nas ("The World Is Yours"), Rakim ("The Saga Begins"), Inspectah Deck ("Trouble Man"), and Kanye West & Jay-Z ("The Joy"), to name just a few. Rock was also the mastermind behind Run-DMC's second-biggest single, "Down with the King," and what is universally considered to be one of the greatest remixes of all time, Public Enemy's "Shut 'Em Down" [Remix]. In hindsight, it's clear that Pete Rock was the bridge from the basic drum-dominated beats of the '80s and the complex productions that we have come to expect recently, meshing the two effortlessly and giving an entire generation of hip-hop fans a taste of jazz without them even realizing it.

4. Kanye West

Geniuses are often eccentric and it's obvious that **Kanye West** is both of those things. If West let his music speak and didn't allow his personality to get in the way, he would probably be even more revered than he already is. Then again, it's clear that his personality is a major essence of his work and removing one would damage the other. The most impressive thing about West's production credits would have to be the incredible diversity of his beats. More than possibly any other producer aside from Dr. Dre, the "Louis Vuitton Don" has changed his sound throughout his career, proving time and again that he can master virtually any subgenre of hip-hop. In his early days, Kanye was the pioneer of the sped-up soul sample that carried Roc-A-Fella at the start of the millennium, providing the foundation for some of the label's best songs. Beanie Sigel ("The Truth," "Nothing Like It"), Freeway ("Turn Out the Lights"), Cam'Ron ("Dead or Alive"), State Property ("Got Nowhere"), and Memphis Bleek ("I Wanna Love You") all benefited from West's groundbreaking style, but it was the producer's work with Jay-Z that elevated that stature of both artists. The two changed the game with *Watch the Throne*, but they changed it a first time a decade earlier. On tracks such as "This Can't Be Life," "Takeover," "Izzo [H.O.V.A.]," "Heart of the City [Ain't No Love]," "Never Change," "'03 Bonnie & Clyde," "Encore," and "Lucifer" the two had an undeniable chemistry and the music was so memorable that it led to countless imitators. While West would soon leave that style behind because it had been exhausted, it would take the rest of the industry another decade to realize the same thing. Of course, Kanye didn't give away all his best material. *The College Dropout*, *Late Registration*, and *Graduation* are all classics in their own way, sounding different from one another, but still resembling the larger overall style. With *808s & Heartbreak*, he created an Auto-Tuned R&B album full of electronica beats that was still critically acclaimed and then brought all of those elements together on *My Beautiful Dark Twisted Fantasy*. The diversity of West's abilities is exemplified by the work he's done for so many various artists. In addition to helping Common return to form on his comeback album *Be*, West has provided the beats for some of hip-hop's biggest names: Lil' Kim ("Don't Mess With Me"), Bump J ("Move Around"), The Game ("Dreams"), Nas ("Poppa Was a Playa"), Scarface ("Guess Who's Back"), Ludacris ("Stand Up"), Consequence ("Grammy Family"), Saigon ("It's Alright"), Rick Ross ("Life Fast, Die young"), and many more. Many people criticize the actions of Kanye West and many people defend them. No one, however, can deny his talent or criticize what he has brought to the world of music. That, in and of itself, should be more than enough of a personality.

3. RZA

The founder of arguably the most original group in music history, **RZA** created more than just music. Wu-Tang became a way of life, inhabiting its own universe and drawing millions into it in the process. From the size of the group, to its unique record contract negotiation, to its logo, to its clothing line, to its slang, to its references, to the music itself, Wu-Tang Clan is the most innovative group in hip-hop history and RZA was at the center of it all. In the group's first five years, from 1993 to 1997, seven albums emanated from the Wu-Tang camp, all of which were produced exclusively by RZA (save for a random track or two) and all seven – two group albums sandwiched around five solo LPs – are considered classics. Most impressively, every album sounds different from the last, suited to fit each artist's strengths or, in the case of the two group projects, to showcase the status of the entire Clan at that point in time. *Enter the Wu-Tang [36 Chambers]* was raw and dirty, purposely made to sound like a demo, with fast-paced beats. The music for Method Man's *Tical* was vague and gloomy, with the momentum being a bit slower than the Clan's debut. Ol' Dirty Bastard's *Return to the 36 Chambers: The Dirty Version* featured production that was disjointed and off kilter, matching O.D.B.'s patented drunken flow. Raekwon's *Only Built 4 Cuban Linx...* was conceived as an audio motion picture and the beats were much more complex, incorporating more of an orchestral sound to serve as a backdrop for the "film." GZA's *Liquid Swords* employs a haunting, atmospheric sound that foretells a sense of doom in the songs. Ghostface Killah's *Ironman* was more intimate, using soul samples to create a more melodic sound without losing any of the grittiness of the previous Wu efforts. Finally, *Wu-Tang Forever* completed the circle of RZA's "five-year plan," with multifaceted and polished beats that bang hard, but sound vastly different from what was offered on *36 Chambers*, particularly the use of sped-up soul music samples, a technique that would be copied years later by Roc-A-Fella producers Kanye West and Just Blaze. Understandably, RZA took a break after *Forever* and the entire group suffered as a result, but he was still able to craft a classic. Not only did he continue to provide the Clan with gems, but he also produced memorable songs for others like Cypress Hill ("Killa Hill Niggas"), AZ ("Doe or Die" [Remix]), Charli Baltimore ("Stand Up"), Big Pun ("Tres Leches [Triboro Trilogy]"), The Game ("Heartbreaker"), Jay-Z & Kanye West ("New Day"), and The Notorious B.I.G. ("Long Kiss Goodnight"). Wu-Tang Clan may no longer be the superpower they were in 1997, but RZA is the reason they were ever in that position in the first place. Without Wu-Tang, hip-hop would not be even close to where it is today. Without RZA and his revolutionary sound, Wu-Tang would never have existed. In other words, RZA was, and is, vital to the genre.

2. DJ Premier

He may have been born and raised in Texas, but **DJ Premier** has been a New Yorker for decades and he became the East Coast's best beat maker in that time. As one-half of the classic duo Gang Starr, Premo was known for laying jazz samples over speaker-splitting drums that create a dichotomy of the music that met somewhere in the middle to create a perfect marriage of the two. He is the only one that can do what he does. His beats sound similar – they are an entire subgenre of their own – but they're always original. That was never truer than during Gang Starr's prime. The fact that it always sounded as if Guru's voice was created strictly to perform over Premier's musical beds only made the music that much greater. Over the course of six albums, there were numerous classic songs – "Mass Appeal," "Royalty," "DWYCK," "Step in the Arena," "You Know My Steez," and more – that all combine the group's best elements: hard drums, stripped-down melodies, Guru's relaxed flow and, most notably, the scratches. For all of his abilities, Premier's most revered technique could be his ability to create a complete chorus only by scratching records (like an actual DJ), usually only records by the artist whose song he was producing, so that the voice on the chorus was almost always the same as that on the verses. Guru was the main beneficiary of Premier's beats and scratches, but he was not alone. Heavyweights such as Nas ("N.Y. State of Mind," Nas Is Like," "Come Get Me"), Rakim ("It's Been a Long Time," "New York [Ya Out There]," "When I B On the Mic"), Jadakiss ("None of Y'all Betta"), Jay-Z ("D'Evils," "So Ghetto"), M.O.P. ("Downtown Swinga," "Follow Instructions"), and The Notorious B.I.G. ("Unbelievable," "Kick in the Door") all benefited from the Premo treatment. While most of those songs represented high points in their careers, most of those artists were already well-known by the time they worked with Premier. To appreciate the full impact of his work, it's more beneficial to look at emcees whose careers were made because of him. Jeru The Damaja's first two albums – *The Sun Rises in the East* and *Wrath of the Math* –were exclusively produced by DJ Premier, critically acclaimed, and spawned a minor hit ("Come Clean" and "Ya Playin' Yaself"), and each reached number 35 on the *Billboard* 200 chart. Since then, Jeru has released three albums with no input from Premier and none of the three have even come close to reaching the charts. That's not a coincidence. Similarly, the duo Group Home's debut album, *Livin' Proof*, was produced almost exclusively by Premier. The LP received rave reviews and even reached number 34 on the *Billboard* R&B/Hip-Hop chart. Although not an enormous commercial success, it became a cult classic, benefitting from word of mouth promotion, particularly for its production. The duo had a falling out with Premier and, as a result, has ostensibly not been heard from since. In hip-hop's early days, the DJ was the star and the MC was present only as a supporting character. Over the years, that dynamic shifted dramatically. However, when it comes to DJ Premier, more often than not, he's still the star of the show.

1. Dr. Dre

Use virtually any metric and the answer will always be the same: **Dr. Dre** is the greatest producer in hip-hop history. Record sales? He has sold more than 20 million albums. Legacy? The graduates of the University of Dre reads like a Hall of Fame lineup – The D.O.C., Ice Cube, Eazy-E, Snoop Dogg, Tha Dogg Pound, Nate Dogg, Eminem, 50 Cent – and his reach extends far beyond hip-hop. In fact, no individual within the music industry has affected popular music more in the past 25 years than Dr. Dre. Influence? Most producers never come close to changing the sound of the entire hip-hop world. The greatest producers maybe do it once. Dre did it three separate times. He introduced "gangster rap" in 1988, "G-Funk" in 1992, and a futuristic combination of the two in 1999. Dr. Dre has released only two solo albums in his career, *The Chronic* and *2001*. They sold a combined 11 million copies in the U.S. alone, spawned the classic hits "Nuthin' but a 'G' Thang," "Dre Day," "Let Me Ride," "Still D.R.E.," "The Next Episode," and "Forgot About Dre," and made its contributors into instant stars. It wasn't the first time. As the producer and sometimes-rapper for N.W.A, he crafted a groundbreaking classic with *Straight Outta Compton* and continued to push the envelope stylistically with the EP *100 Miles and Runnin'* and the full-length *Niggaz4Life*. In spite of his success with those projects, an argument could be made that Dre's best work comes when he remains behind the boards. In the late '80s, he produced the critically-acclaimed debuts of both Eazy-E (*Eazy Duz It*) and The D.O.C. (*No One Can Do It Better*). Five years later, he produced Snoop Doggy Dogg's own debut, *Doggystyle*, an effort that was even more intricate than *The Chronic* and turned Snoop into the biggest star in music at the time. Six years after that, Dre discovered a white emcee from Detroit with bleached blonde hair and a penchant for violent, yet witty lyrics, producing Eminem's "My Name Is," the song that made him a household name, as well as the other two singles from Em's debut, "Role Model," and "Guilty Conscience." He executive produced every one of Eminem's albums and supplied the beats to some of his more popular songs – "Kill You," "The Real Slim Shady," "Business," "Say What You Say," "Never Enough," "Mosh," "Just Lose It," "Ass Like That" – before producing the entirety of his 2009 comeback disc, *Relapse*. And it wasn't just his own label's artists with whom Dre collaborated. Throughout his career, Andre Young has worked with the best in the game: 2Pac ("California Love"), Nas ("Nas Is Coming"), Scarface ("Game Over"), Warren G ("Game Don't Wait" [Remix]), Ice Cube ("Hello"), Xzibit ("X"), Eve ("Let Me Blow Your Mind"), Mary J. Blige ("Family Affair"), The Firm ("Phone Tap"), Busta Rhymes ("Break Ya Neck"), Jay-Z ("Lost One," "30 Something"), 50 Cent ("In Da Club," "If I Can't"), The Game ("Westside Story," "Hate It or Love It") and Raekwon ("Catalina"). He's also won a total of six Grammy Awards, three of which came exclusively for production. Long after he is gone, Dre's effect on music will continue on and will only stop once there is no longer of genre of music called hip-hop. Dr. Dre is the greatest producer in hip-hop history and he has the sales, the artists, the influence, and the classics to prove it.

<u>Honorable Mentions</u>

Q-Tip

Havoc

J. Dilla

2. THE BEST DUOS/GROUPS OF ALL TIME

10. Gang Starr

The DJ/MC combo is the foundation of hip-hop music. Everything else is built upon that relationship and few groups mastered it as well as Guru and DJ Premier, collectively known as **Gang Starr**. Guru's lyrics, known for their introspection and intelligence, were always delivered in his trademark monotone cadence, as he never had to resort to screaming or other gimmicks to be heard, and they seemed tailor-made for DJ Premier's crushing drums and jazzy melodies. The two joined forces in 1989, a time of transition in hip-hop, when one era was ending and another was just beginning. Their debut, *No More Mr. Nice Guy*, introduced the duo and, on cuts like "Words I Manifest," gave a glimpse into what was to come later, but it was their second effort, 1991's *Step In the Arena*, that found Gang Starr truly hitting its stride, as evidenced on "Who's Gonna Take The Weight?," "Just to Get a Rep," and the album's title track. A year later came *Daily Operation*, a darker effort that embodied the grittier sounds of early-to-mid '90s New York hip-hop and found Guru expanding his subject matter to include classic boasting ("I'm the Man"), the deterioration of friendship ("Take It Personal"), the hopelessness of inner-city violence ("Soliloquy of Chaos"), and failed relationships ("Ex Girl to the Next Girl"). In 1994, the group released *Hard to Earn*, a much denser and less melodic album that was built around the classic DJ Premier sound and presented a slightly more aggressive Guru, as showcased on "Now You're Mine," "Tonz 'O' Gunz," "Speak Ya Clout," and the album's undisputed high point, the Nice & Smooth-assisted party cut, "DWYCK." Following a four year hiatus in which the two focused on other projects, they returned for the emotional *Moment of Truth*, the duo's magnum opus. By this time, Gang Starr had already established themselves as heavyweights in the genre, but their fifth album, their only studio project to achieve gold status, elevated them even higher. Both Guru and Premier were at their peak and it showed throughout the album, from "Royalty," to "Above the Clouds," to "Betrayal," to perhaps their greatest work, "You Know My Steez," on which Guru shows off his wordplay: *"The beat is sinister, Primo makes you relax/I'm like the minister, when I be lacing the wax/I be bringing salvation through the way that I rap/And you know, and I know, I'm nice like that/Work through worldly problems, I got the healing power/When the mic's within my reach/I'm feeling more power/Stealing at least three minutes of every rap radio hour/It's often easier for one to give advice/Than it is for a person to run one's own life/That's why I can't be caught up in all the hype/I keep my soul tight and let these lines takes flight/The apparatus gets blessed, and suckers get put to rest/No more of the unpure, I got the cure for this mess/The wackness is spreading like the plague/MC's lucked up and got paid but still can't make the fucking grade/How many times are wannabe's gonna lie?/Yo, they must wanna fry, they can't touch the knowledge I personify/I travel through the darkness carrying my torch/The illest soldier, when I'm holding down the fort/You know my steez."* The duo split following one more album, 2003's *The Ownerz*, and Guru's death in 2010 prevented any sort of reunion, but for a decade-and-a-half, Gang Starr provided intelligent, uncompromising hip-hop that elevated the art form and made them legends in the genre. No one can take that away from them.

9. The Roots

There is a typical formula in hip-hop: a producer creates a beat with a drum machine and then an emcee raps over it. Philadelphia's **The Roots**, however, are not the typical group. Since 1993, the band has been incorporating live instrumentation into its music, being one of the few East Coast hip-hop acts to feature a drummer, guitarist, and keyboardist both in the studio and on stage. Like all great groups, The Roots push traditional boundaries, both musically and lyrically, winning four Grammys in the process. The urban equivalent of U2, every Roots album is different and original. The band's early work – *Organix* and *Do You Want More?!!!??!* – saw them presenting and perfecting their unique brand of tunes. Next came the commercial breakthroughs – *Illadelph Halflife* and *Things Fall Apart* – before several group members left the band. With a revised lineup, the remaining albums – *Phrenology*, *The Tipping Point*, *Game Theory*, *Rising Down*, *How I Got Over*, *Wake Up!* (with John Legend), *Betty Wright: The Movie* (with Betty Wright), and *Undun* – sounded different than previous efforts, but continued to gain critical praise and add to the band's legacy, due to the continual presence of the band's original founders, Questlove and Black Thought. Questlove, the band's drummer, acts as its musical director and lead producer, seamlessly mixing neo-soul, jazz, and funk elements with his ever-present drums. Behind the microphone, Black Thought's flawless flow and intelligent lyrics are the perfect complement to the originality of the music. Nowhere is this better exemplified than on the Erykah Badu and Eve-assisted "You Got Me," which nabbed the group its first Grammy. Over the slow instrumentation and powerful drums, Thought intends his verses to reach the unenlightened through a love story: "*Somebody told me that this planet was small/We used to live in the same building on the same floor/And never met before/Until I'm overseas on tour/And peep this Ethiopian queen from Philly taking classes abroad/She's studying film and photo, flash, focus, record/Said she working on a flick/And could my clique do the score?/She said she loved my show in Paris at Élysée Montmartre/And that I stepped off the stage and took a piece of her heart/We knew from the start that/Things Fall Apart, intentions shatter/She's like 'That shit don't matter'/When I get home, get at her/Through letter, phone, whatever/Let's link, let's get together/Shit you think not, think the Thought went home and forgot/Time passed, we back in Philly, now she up in my spot/Telling me the things I'm telling her is* making her hot/Started building with her constantly 'round the clock/Now she in my world like hip-hop." From releasing a debut album independently to winning Grammys to becoming the house band for *Late Night with Jimmy Fallon*, the rise of The Roots is astounding.

8. EPMD

Few groups have had the impact and influence of **EPMD**. Along with Rick Rubin, Marley Marl and The Bomb Squad, they were an integral part of hip-hop moving away from its basic disco and electronic origins and towards the funk and rock-based approach that would dominate the genre for the next decade. Beginning in 1988 with their gold-certified classic debut *Strictly Business*, Erick Sermon and Parish Smith changed the game with their music that was aimed squarely at the city with sample-heavy beats and lyrics full of punchlines while also setting fashion trends with their hoodies and bucket hats. Over the next three years, they would join Def Jam, release three more gold albums – *Unfinished Business*, *Business as Usual*, and *Business Never Personal* – and introduce their protégés, the Hit Squad, featuring future stars such as Keith Murray, Redman, and Das EFX, as well as K-Solo and DJ Scratch, to the world. Following an acrimonious breakup in 1993, the duo reunited in 1997 and released two more gold albums – *Back in Business* and *Out of Business* – as well as a greatest hits album and one final effort, *We Mean Business*. The forefathers of New York City streetwise rap, Smith and Sermon had incredible chemistry that led to the numerous classic cuts: "You Gots to Chill," "So Wat Cha Sayin'," "Gold Digger," "Rampage," "Crossover," "Head Banger," and "Da Joint." Their first single, "It's My Thing," is the perfect encapsulation of what the group was and why they were so important: "[Sermon] *The E-R-I-C-K is my name, I spell/Thanks to the clientele, yo, I rock well/I'm not an MC who talking all that junk/About who can beat who, sounding like a punk/I just get down and I go for mine/Say 'check one-two,' and run down the line.* [Smith] *To the average MC, I'm known as The Terminator/Funky beat maker, new jack exterminator/Destroy and employ, when your rhymes are not void/Never* sweating your girl (*Why P?*) *'Cause she's a skeezoid/When I'm on the scene, I always rock the spot/I grab the steel with the crown on top..."* While EPMD's prime lasted only four years and spawned just four albums before temporarily disbanding, all four were classics that inspired an entire generation of emcees and producers to create music that spoke to the streets. In fact, much of the greatest hip-hop music of the past two decades either samples or borrows heavily from EPMD and that is the ultimate proof of their importance to the culture.

7. Outkast

They say that opposites attract and no group is comprised of opposites like Atlanta-based **Outkast**. Big Boi had an honestly straightforward style with a serious and monotone delivery aimed at the streets while André 3000 was the unconventional one with quotable lyrics, an unrivaled imagination, and a style that could fit any beat just like water can fit any apparatus. Winners of a combined five Grammys, the duo released six studio albums, each of which sold at least one million copies and garnered critical praise. Outkast was the rare southern act of the mid-'90s that promoted artistic integrity and multifaceted lyrics over the simplistic and bling-obsessed style of No Limit and Cash Money Records. The most original and unpredictable mainstream group in hip-hop history, they announced their arrival with *Southernplayalisticadillacmuzik*, a fairly uninspired but well-executed debut. It wasn't until 1996's *ATLiens* that the duo began to embrace their weirdness and eccentricities and living up to the album's title with most of the tracks sounding as if they were created in outer space. Their following two efforts, *Aquemini* and *Stankonia*, sold two and four million copies respectively and solidified the group's standing as one of the most popular but still well-respected groups in all of popular music at the turn of the millennium. This duality was nowhere more evident than on "Ms. Jackson," the relatable track dedicated to a disappointed mother-in-law: "[André 3000] *Ten times out of nine, now if I'm lying, find/The quickest muzzle, throw it on my mouth and I'll decline/King meets queen, then the puppy love thing, together* *dream/'Bout that crib with the Goodyear swing/On the oak tree, I hope we feel like this forever/Forever, forever/Ever, forever, ever?/Forever never seems that long until you're grown/And notice that the day by day ruler can't be too wrong/Ms. Jackson, my intentions were good, I wish I could/Become a magician to abracadabra all the sadder/Thoughts of me, thoughts of she, thoughts of he/Asking what happened to the feeling that her and me/Had, I pray so much about it need some knee pads/It happened for a reason, on.e can't be mad/So know this, know that everything's cool/And yes, I will be present on the first day of school/And graduation."* That success eventually led to 2003's *Speakerboxxx/The Love Below*. Two solo albums packaged together, it won the coveted Grammy for Album of the Year and is technically the most successful hip-hop album of all time, selling over 11 million copies (counted twice since it was a double album). Despite the success, the album was a clear sign that the duo's relationship was fractured, a fact further proven on the disappointing *Idlewild*, the group's final album that also served as a soundtrack to the film of the same name in which both starred. Ultimately, their differences, which had been the group's greatest strength, became too much to overcome and the two went their separate ways and, to this point, have not recorded since. Not only were they different from each other, they were different from the rest of the industry. With a catalog that includes five gold and one platinum single and memorable tracks including "B.O.B.," "Two Dope Boyz (In a Cadillac)," "The Way You Move," "Rosa Parks," "Player's Ball," "So Fresh, So Clean," "Roses," "Hey Ya!," and the aforementioned "Ms. Jackson," Outkast showed that it's possible to be great simply by being yourself.

6. Beastie Boys

Very few musical acts of any sort have the same permanence as the **Beastie Boys**. Beginning as a hardcore punk band in the late '70s, the trio of Ad-Rock, MCA, and Mike D found their groove when they transitioned to hip-hop in the early-to-mid-'80s. After befriending Rick Rubin, they released their debut, *Licensed to Ill*, in late 1986 on Def Jam Recordings.

The album was a breakthrough for both the group and the genre, becoming the first hip-hop album to reach the top spot on the *Billboard* 200 chart and the best-selling rap album of the decade with over nine million copies sold. Following their departure from Def Jam, they took their artistry to another level in 1989, releasing the Dust Brothers-produced *Paul's Boutique*, a momentous album that was not as commercially successful (though it did eventually reach double platinum status), but was far more important than their debut. In the '90s, the group released three albums – *Check Your Head*, *Ill Communication*, and *Hello Nasty* – each of which sold more than two million copies and were all sonically different from one another, showcasing the Beasties' talents and their penchant for experimentation. Three more albums followed – 2004's *To the Five Boroughs*, 2007's instrumental album *The Mix-Up* (for which they won a Grammy), and 2011's *Hot Sauce Committee Part Two* – further expanding the trio's musicality while still remaining, at heart, hip-hop heads. This combination of deft lyricism over unconventional beats is best exemplified on 1992's "So What'cha Want": "[Ad Rock] *Well just plug me in just like I was Eddie Harris/You're eating crazy cheese like you'd think I'm from Paris/You know I get fly, you think I get high/You know that I'm gone and I'm a tell you all why/*[Mike D] *So tell me who are you dissing, maybe I'm missing/The reason that you're smiling or wilding, so listen/In my head I just want to take 'em down/Imagination set loose and I'm gonna shake 'em down/*[MCA] *Let it flow like a mud slide/When I get on, I like to ride and glide/I've got depth of perception in my text y'all/I get props at my mention 'cause I vex y'all/* [Ad Rock] *So what'cha what'cha what'cha want? (what'cha want?)/I get so funny with my money that you flaunt/I said where'd you get your information from, huh?/You think that you can front when revelation comes?/(Yeah, you can't front on that)/*[Mike D]*Well they call me Mike D, the ever loving man/I'm like Spoonie Gee (whoo ooh), I'm the metro-politician (yeah-yeah-yeah-yeah!)/You scream and you holler, about my Chevy Impala/But the sweat is getting wetter than the ring around your collar/*[MCA] *But like a dream, I'm flowing without no stopping/Sweeter than a cherry pie with Reddi-wip topping/Going from mic to mic, kicking it wall to wall/Well, I'll be calling out you people like a casting call...*" From "Hey Ladies" to "Make Some

Noise," and from "(You Gotta) Fight for Your Right (To Party!)" to "Sabotage," they made hit songs for more than 20 years, right up until the death of MCA in 2012. While many now take the Beastie Boys for granted, it is nothing short of remarkable that three white Jewish kids became one of the most successful acts in hip-hop history, both commercially and critically, with the most varied catalog in popular music, eventually leading to an induction into the Rock and Roll Hall of Fame. To sell over 40 million albums worldwide while keeping the respect of your peers is a rare feat and you can't front on that.

5. A Tribe Called Quest

There are very few hip-hop groups that deserve to have a documentary made about them. Fewer still would warrant that it would be directed by a white Hollywood actor. Then again, **A Tribe Called Quest** is not the typical group. From 1990 – 1998, Q-Tip, Phife Dawg, Ali Shaheed Muhammad, and Jarobi presented their sound and it was a sound that had never been heard before. A combination of classic jazz and classic hip-hop, it created a new middle ground between the different facets of the genre that had evolved over the years and inspired future producers such as Pharrell Williams, J. Dilla, and Kanye West to experiment in their own careers. Culturally, the group was authentic and original, initially wearing traditional African garb to show their ties to the Universal Zulu Nation before ultimately crafting their own style that was different from every other act at the time. They were also founding members of the Native Tongues, a collective including De La Soul, Jungle Brothers, Chi-Ali, Black Sheep, Monie Love, Queen Latifah, and Leaders of the New School, that were similar in their outlook and approach to music. While Tribe's debut, *People's Instinctive Travels and the Paths of Rhythm*, featured renowned tracks like "Can I Kick It?," "I Left My Wallet in El Segundo," and "Bonita Applebum," it wasn't until their second album, *The Low End Theory*, that they became a musical juggernaut. Phife and Tip, the two vocalists, were a study in contrasts and that relationship shone through on their sophomore effort. They could not have been less alike musically. They had completely different voices, styles, deliveries, cadence, and attitude, all of which created the perfect yin and yang balance on the microphone. *Low End* was a triumph in every facet, from the rhymes, to the hooks, to the beats, exemplified on cuts like "Buggin' Out," the classic posse cut, "Scenario," and perhaps the group's best song, "Check the Rhime," which saw the two emcees trading words effortlessly: [Phife Dawg] *Back in days on the boulevard of Linden/We used to kick routines and the presence was fitting/It was I, the Phifer/*[Q-Tip] A*nd me, The Abstract/The rhymes were so rumping that the brothers rode the 'zack/*[Phife Dawg] *Yo Tip, do you recall when we used to rock/Those fly routines on your cousin's block?/* [Q-Tip] *Um, let me see/Damn I can't remember/I receive the message and you will play the sender/*[P] *You on point, Tip?/*[Q-Tip] *All the time, Phife/*[Phife Dawg] *You on point,Tip?/* [Q-Tip] *Yeah, all the time, Phife/*[Phife Dawg] *You on point, Tip?/* [Q-Tip] *Yo, all the time, Phife/*[Phife Dawg] *So play the resurrector and give the dead some life/*[Q-Tip] *Okay, if knowledge is the key then just show me the lock/Got the scrawny legs, but I move just like Lou Brock/With speed/I'm agile, plus I'm worth your while/One hundred percent intelligent black child/My optic presentation sizzles the retina/How far must I go to gain respect? Um.../Well, it's kind of simple, just remain your own/Or you'll be crazy sad and alone/Industry rule number four thousand and eighty/Record company people are shady...*" Two years later, they surpassed that achievement with *Midnight Marauders*, the group's most successful and, arguably, greatest album. "Award Tour" was a major hit, but other songs like "Lyrics to Go" and "Oh My God" saw Tribe at their pinnacle, creating a masterpiece that still holds up nearly twenty years later. Their final two albums – *Beats, Rhymes and Life* and *The Love Movement* – suffered from group turmoil, Phife's decision to move out of the New York, and Q-Tip and Ali's decision to include J. Dilla in the production process (under the collective name The Ummah), a decision that radically changed the group's sound and disrupted their chemistry. While a notch below their earlier work, these albums were still better than the vast majority of releases during that time and would have been lauded if not for Tribe setting the bar so high with the first three albums. When they disbanded in 1998, it was a sad day in hip-hop and while they occasionally reunite to tour, it is doubtful that they'll ever record a full album again, which is unfortunate because music needs more groups like A Tribe Called Quest.

4. N.W.A

The five-man collective known as **N.W.A** was called the "world's most dangerous group" for a reason. Ice Cube, Eazy-E, MC Ren, DJ Yella, and Dr. Dre brilliantly expressed the pent-up aggression they felt living in Compton, California through angry, violent rhymes backed by loud, brash music. Since its inception, hip-hop had been dominated by individuals from New York, espousing their backgrounds and the situations that they encountered in their lives. Meanwhile, there was an entirely different, though no less impactful, kind of urban hopelessness that existed on the other side of the country that was not being reported in the culture. N.W.A changed that. Instead of boots and jeans, they wore khakis and Converse All-Stars. They wore black Raiders hats and rapped about drive-by shootings. When it was released, *Straight Outta Compton* was an album that literally shocked the world. Brutally honest, vividly violent, and in-your-face from beginning to end, it became an instant masterpiece. The singles received virtually no radio or video airplay yet the album sold more than two million records and forced the assistant director of the FBI to write them a letter condemning their music. Ice Cube departed after one album, and while the group did suffer, they endured, releasing an EP (*100 Miles and Runnin'*) and an LP (*Niggaz4Life*), the latter of which reached the top spot on the *Billboard* 200, a staggering feat for a group that many had tried to ban just two years earlier. The group would disband shortly thereafter, but the N.W.A legacy would continue on for years to come. Ice Cube, Eazy-E, and Dr. Dre all became extremely successful solo artists and launched the careers of other stars. Following N.W.A's lead, an entire generation of emcees moved away from battle rapping and began incorporating violent imagery and stories of living in the 'hood into their rhymes. Songs like "Straight Outta Compton," "Fuck tha Police," and "Real Niggaz Don't Die" would become the basis for much of the music heard throughout the 1990s, particularly from the west coast. An underrated, but still very key, element to the group was its storytelling ability, showcased on songs like "Dopeman" [Remix], "Just Don't Bite It," "Alwayz into Somethin'," and "Gangsta Gangsta," on which Ice Cube explains his team's opinions on social subjects before launching into a story about meeting girls and engaging in shootouts: *"Since I was a youth, I smoked weed out/Now I'm the motherfucker that you read about/Taking a life or two, that's what the hell I do/You don't like how I'm living? Well fuck you!/This is a gang, and I'm in it/My man Dre will fuck you up in a minute/With a right, left, right, left you're toothless/And then you say, 'Goddamn they Ruthless!'/Everywhere we go they say 'Damn!/N W A's fucking up the program/And then you realize, we don't care/We don't just say no, we too busy saying 'Yeah!'/To drinking straight out the eight bottle/Do I look like a motherfucking role model?/To a kid looking up to me: Life ain't nothin' but bitches and money..."* In retrospect, it's hard to imagine a musical landscape where Dr. Dre and Ice Cube are unknowns or where rapping about drug deals and street violence warrants an investigation from the Secret Service, but that was the reality before N.W.A arrived on the scene and that alone is more than enough to explain their importance to the culture.

3. Public Enemy

There was a time when hip-hop was the social conscious of the young, inner-city community. With nowhere else to turn to speak the truth, they used music to get their message out to the masses. In the late '80s and early '90s, there were several groups that fit this description, such as X-Clan and Poor Righteous Teachers, but one group was far more important – and far greater – than the rest. **Public Enemy** was at the forefront of sociopolitical rap, using their pulpit as a way to enlighten listeners, shed light on cultural issues, and motivate a generation to become more socially active. Most importantly, they made it sound so good. Each member brought a unique skill that, when taken together, created beautiful chaos. Over innovatively intricate yet raucous beats provided by the Bomb Squad, Chuck D's powerful voice was like a megaphone, forcing everyone within earshot to absorb every word, while Flavor Flav, the greatest hype man in history, chimed in with ad-libs and jokes, and Terminator X played the role of DJ. When their debut album, *Yo! Bum Rush the Show*, dropped in 1987, it introduced a much more serious, and hostile, approach to music, eschewing melodies and ignoring traditional song structures without ever taking their foot off the gas pedal. A year later, they would release the breathtaking *It Takes a Nation of Millions to Hold Us Back* and hip-hop would never be the same. A perfect album from start to finish, it employed extremely fast beats that stacked samples on top of one another and featured Chuck D fearlessly playing the role of both a teacher and an entertainer, exploring the problems of inner-city youth, railing against a corrupt political system, and promoting the American pro-black movement. Their reign atop the hip-hop world would continue over the course of two more excellent albums, the deeper *Fear of a Black Planet* and the return-to-form frenzy of *Apocalypse '91...The Enemy Strikes Black*. From 1987 – 1991, P.E. was responsible for a multitude of classic songs including, "Fight the Power," "Black Steel in the Hour of Chaos," "Can't Truss It," "Rebel Without a Pause," "Miuzi Weighs a Ton," "Don't Believe the Hype," "Shut 'em Down," "Night of the Living Baseheads," "911 Is a Joke," "Burn Hollywood Burn," "Bring the Noise," and "By the Time I Get to Arizona." This last song, in reference to the state refusing to recognize the Martin Luther King, Jr. holiday, was a quintessential P.E. song, complete with a hard rock-inspired beat and some of the harshest lyrics of Chuck D's illustrious career, all presented in an original, staccato flow that would have stymied a lesser emcee: *"Yeah, he appear to be fair/The cracker over there/He try to keep it yesteryear/The good ol' days/The same ol' ways/That kept us dying/Yes, you, me, myself and I'n/-Deed/What he need is a nosebleed/Read/Between the lines/Then you see the lie/Politically planned/But understand/That's all she wrote/When we see the real side/That hide/Behind the vote/They can't understand/Why he the man/I'm singing 'bout a **King**/They don't like it/When I decide to mic it/Wait/I'm waiting for the date/For the man who demands respect/Cause he was great/C'mon/I'm on the one mission/To get a politician/To honor/Or he's a goner/By the time I get to Arizona!"* While their later efforts did not have the same impact as their first four albums, Public Enemy's place in history is cemented. In addition to their trailblazing music and political stances, the group was also at the forefront of several music trends. They were one of the first hip-hop acts to sell out shows around the globe, bringing the genre to every corner of the world. They were also influential in introducing the subgenre of rap metal by collaborating with heavy metal band Anthrax for a remix of "Bring the Noise." Finally, they embraced the opportunities that the internet had to offer, voluntarily releasing their music through mp3s as far back as 1999, long before iTunes existed. For about a decade, it seemed as if they were ahead of the curve in every facet of the business. In short, Public Enemy's importance on the entire music industry cannot be overstated.

2. Run-D.M.C.

More than any other group or artist, **Run-D.M.C.** was responsible for hip-hop's growth from neighborhood activity to mainstream musical genre. The forefathers of modern hip-hop, Run, Jam Master Jay, and DMC almost singlehandedly proved that their contributions could be as viable, successful, and artistic as other musicians. They were trendsetters in every possible way. Musically, they were the first artists to create more forceful hip-hop with sparse beats that brought attention to their simple yet catchy lyrics and were aimed at getting people to bob their heads rather than dance, an element of the music that continues to this day. They even broke down traditional musical barriers through their collaboration with the rock band Aerosmith on "Walk This Way." The sounds of artists like the Beastie Boys, Public Enemy, and even N.W.A in the mid-to-late '80s were directly influenced by the work of Run-D.M.C. Visually, they rejected the ostentatious, disco-inspired stage costumes worn by artists like Afrika Bambaataa and Melle Mel, choosing instead to wear more comfortable clothes that could be seen in most American cities – fedoras, t-shirts, leather jackets, and jeans, all adorned with a thick gold chain. Furthermore, their style of wearing Adidas sneakers without laces became their signature trademark, leading to a hit single,

"My Adidas," and an endorsement deal with the company, a first for a hip-hop act. That was only the beginning. Run-D.M.C. achieved many firsts for hip-hop artists, including being the first rappers to appear on the cover of *Rolling Stone*, the first to have their video shown on MTV, and the first to have an album reach gold, platinum, *and* multiplatinum status. Their first album, *Run-D.M.C.*, was a revelation, introducing a brand new sound and relegating everything that came before it as obsolete. The first album to reach gold status, it featured the seminal tracks, "It's Like That," "Sucker M.C.'s," and "Rock Box," the last of which was the first rap video aired on MTV in 1984. A year later, they released the first platinum album in hip-hop history, *King of Rock*, but it was their third album that firmly established Run-D.M.C. as the face of hip-hop and changed the culture forever. Released in 1986, *Raising Hell* is an undisputed classic, recorded when the group was at their absolute apex and boasting the instant classics, "Peter Piper," "You Be Illin'," "My Adidas," "It's Tricky," and the "Walk This Way" redux that featured Aerosmith. The album was a triumph for the entire genre, selling more than three million copies and becoming the standard for every album that followed it over the next several years. It would be the high point for the group. The follow-up, *Tougher Than Leather*, featured the song, "Mary, Mary," a track that prominently included a sample of the popular '60s band The Monkeys and showed that Run and DMC had not lost a step: "[Run] *Now/This girl Mary I knew so well/I met her on the road in a fly hotel/High on the heels and never failed/*[DMC] *Clubs and the pubs is where she dwelled/*[Run] *Story about Mary was well to tell/She seemed to scheme for a dream to sell/She spent a night locked in a cell/I knew Mary well cause she's Raising Hell/*[sample] *Mary, Mary/*[Run & DMC] *Why ya' buggin'?/*[sample] *Mary, Mary/*[Run & DMC] *I Need ya' huggin'/*[DMC] *It's not Mary who was quite contrary/Talking 'bout Mary who was always in a hurry/The things she needed were necessary/She did not need a busted cherry/True and blue just like a blueberry/Ask if she's crazy and I'll say very/Living in a house that's out on the prairie/I worry about Mary 'cause Mary is scary!*" The album reached platinum status and also includes the tracks "Beats to the Rhyme," and "Run's House," but it failed to match its predecessor's success. Three more albums, *Back from Hell*, *Down with the King,* and

Crown Royal, would follow, but it was clear that their time had come and gone. After the murder of Jam Master Jay, Run and DMC jointly announced the retirement of the group, vowing to never perform under that moniker again. It was a sad end to the most important and groundbreaking act in hip-hop history.

1. Wu-Tang Clan

When the Wu-Tang Clan burst onto the scene in 1993, they annihilated every standard and preconceived notion of what a hip-hop group should be. Too large (nine members), too weird (they rhymed about chess and kung fu), and too unpolished (their first single had no chorus and sounded like a demo), no one would have guessed that they would have released a successful album, let alone become the biggest hip-hop act in the world less than five years later. When *Enter the Wu-Tang [36 Chambers]* was released, it was unlike anything that had ever been heard in the history of hip-hop. Standing in stark contrast to the sophisticated and polished sound of others, *36 Chambers* was like opening a time capsule, with samples that crackled and straightforward rhymes that seemed to go on forever. From the power of the first single, "Protect Ya Neck," to the street imagery of "C.R.E.A.M.," to the star-making cuts of "Method Man," and "Shame on a Nigga," Wu's debut introduced a new group with a new sound and a popular new logo. It also introduced a new business model. At a time when artists were still controlled by their record labels, RZA negotiated a contract that signed the group to Loud Records but still allowed all nine members – Method Man (Def Jam), Ol' Dirty Bastard (Elektra), Raekwon (Loud), GZA (Geffen), Ghostface Killah (Epic), RZA (Gee Street), Inspectah Deck (Loud), U-God (Priority), and Masta Killa (Nature Sounds) – to sign solo contracts with any label of their choosing. When he formed the group, RZA promised all of them that he would make them the number one act in rap within the span of five years as long as they agreed to not question his decisions. He called it the "five year plan" and it worked to perfection. Wu-Tang released a second album, *Wu-Tang Forever*, in 1997, five years after the group's formation in 1992. In between the two group albums, five members each released solo albums that were exclusively produced by RZA, Method Man's *Tical*, Ol' Dirty Bastard's *Return to the 36 Chambers: The Dirty Version*, Raekwon's *Only Built 4 Cuban Linx...*, GZA's *Liquid Swords*, and Ghostface Killah's *Ironman*, all of which are considered classics and included some of the most recognizable songs of the '90s: "Bring the Pain," "Shimmy Shimmy Ya," "Ice Cream," "4th Chamber," and "All That I Got Is You." As a result, *Wu-Tang Forever* was one of the most anticipated releases in music history and it did not disappoint, debuting at number one on the *Billboard* 200 chart and reaching quadruple platinum status in the U.S. alone. A double album that showcased all nine members, as well as close affiliate Cappadonna, *Wu-Tang Forever* dominated the summer of 1997, led by the first single, "Triumph." Like "Protect Ya Neck" before it, "Triumph" had no chorus or melody, just eight members and Cappadonna spitting verses with an introduction and interlude by Ol' Dirty Bastard, but it still garnered heavy airplay on radio stations. The song's first verse, by Inspectah Deck, is one of the greatest verses ever recorded: "*I bomb atomically/Socrates' philosophies and hypotheses/Can't define how I be dropping these/Mockeries/Lyrically perform armed robbery/Flee with the lottery/Possibly they spotted me/Battle-scarred shogun, explosion when my pen hits/Tremendous/ultra-violet shine blind forensics/I inspect you, through the future see millennium/Killer Bees sold fifty gold, sixty platinum/Shackling the masses with drastic rap tactics/Graphic displays melt the steel like blacksmiths/Black Wu jackets, queen bees ease the guns in/Rumble with patrolmen, tear gas laced the function/Heads by the score, take flight, incite a war/Chicks hit the floor, diehard fans demand more/Behold the bold soldier, control the globe slowly/Proceed to blow, swinging swords like Shinobi/Stomp grounds and pound footprints in solid rock/Wu got it locked, performing live on your hottest block.*" With the success of the album, the Clan was undoubtedly the biggest act in the genre. RZA's promise had come true and his plan was complete. That would be the group's pinnacle. Going forward, RZA would delegate much of the work he had handled previously, most notably no longer exclusively producing each solo album, which resulted in the brand becoming a bit diluted, but the group has toured successfully for several years and notable releases still coming from members, like the group's third release as a whole, *The W*, Ghostface's *Supreme Clientele*, GZA's collobative effort with Cypress Hill's DJ Muggs, *Grandmasters*, and Raekwon's long awaited sequel to *Cuban Linx…* They now have a few blemishes on their record, but Wu-Tang dominated every aspect of hip-hop, beyond just music: slang ("Shaolin" for Staten Island), a clothing line (Wu Wear), video games (*Wu-Tang: Shaolin Style*), books (*The Tao of Wu*), and more. They even make baby clothes and bibs adorned with the Clan's logo. Considering their longevity – they're still touring and making music twenty years after *36 Chambers* – and influence – their affiliates have had had successful careers, their classic albums begot classic albums, virtually every artist of the past two decades has somehow borrowed from the Clan, and producers like Kanye West cite RZA as their main inspiration – it's clear that they were more than just a musical group. They created a way of life with their very own universe. Without a doubt, Wu-Tang Clan is the greatest hip-hop group ever.

Honorable Mentions

De La Soul

Mobb Deep

Bone Thugs-N-Harmony

UGK

1. THE BEST ARTISTS OF ALL TIME

10. LL Cool J

Possibly the most dichotomous artist in history, **LL Cool J** has been balancing hard-edged battle rhymes with compassionate lyrics aimed at the softer sex since 1985. The first artist to release an album on Def Jam Recordings, James Todd Smith made a splash with *Radio*, his Rick Rubin-produced debut that introduced Rubin's sparse, stripped-down beats as well as Cool J's originality on tracks such as "Rock the Bells," "I Need a Beat," and "I Can't Live Without My Radio." The album sold more than a million copies, making LL one of hip-hop's first stars, and allowing him to be the first rapper featured on *American Bandstand*. Two years later, he released *Bigger and Deffer*, the first album that would feature his trademark style of balancing both sides of his persona, with the boastful "I'm Bad," and hip-hop's first ballad, "I Need Love." The album went double platinum, but after a third effort, *Walking with a Panther,* that also went platinum but was filled with almost strictly softer cuts like "Big Ole Butt," and "I'm That Type of Guy," many believed that LL had lost his edge and was no longer capable of making battle raps. As would become his style, Ladies Love Cool James answered his critics with a vengeance, releasing the critically acclaimed *Mama Said Knock You Out*, a return to form with "Around the Way Girl," the response to Kool Moe Dee, "To Da Break of Dawn," "The Boomin' System," and the album's title track, on which he exclaimed: *"Don't call it a comeback/I've been here for* *years/Rocking my peers and putting suckers in fear/Making the tears/Rain down like a monsoon/Listen to the bass go boom!/Explosion!/Overpowering/Over the competition, I'm towering/Wrecking shop/When I drop/These lyrics that'll make you call the cops/Don't you dare/Stare/You better move/Don't ever compare/Me to the rest that'll all get sliced and diced/Competition's paying the price!"* Produced entirely by Marley Marl, the album sold 2.7 million copies, bolstered by a stirring performance by Cool J on MTV's first hip-hop edition of *Unplugged*. Following a failed attempt to emulate the "gangster rap" style that was popular at the time with 1993's *14 Shots to the Dome*, LL once again returned to his roots two years later on the double platinum, Grammy-nominated *Mr. Smith*, balancing "Hey Lover," "Doin' It," and "Loungin'," with "I Shot Ya," and "Get Da Drop On 'Em." Released ten years to the week after his debut, *Mr. Smith* cemented Cool J's skills and vaulted him into the conversation as one of the greats. Though it did go platinum, his next album, *Phenomenon*, was a disappointment, known best for the issues created during the recording of the posse cut "4, 3, 2, 1," which saw the beginning of the feud between LL and upstart Canibus. After Canibus dropped a strong diss track, "Second Round K.O.," few believed that Cool J could recover. Just as he had in 1990, he responded with "The Ripper Strikes Back," a scathing response that played a major role in Canibus becoming one of the biggest disappointments in history, as well as reinforcing Cool J's battle rap legacy. Since then, he has released five albums, the first four of which reached gold status. Most were a bit softer than previous efforts and focused on his legacy and career with Def Jam, evidenced by their titles: *G.O.A.T.*, *10*, *The DEFinition* (which was nominated for a Grammy), *Todd Smith*, and *Exit 13*. While LL has focused on acting in recent years and is no longer one of the top in the business – a fact he would blame on changes in Def Jam's hierarchy and lack of promotion for his albums – his longevity is unmatched and twelve consecutive gold or platinum albums has been achieved by few artists in history. With thirteen albums, two greatest hits albums, two Grammy Awards, and more than 25 million albums sold worldwide under his belt, LL Cool J has been a hip-hop icon for a quarter-century. Moreover, his six gold and two platinum singles are further proof that he knows how to make songs that appeal to the masses. What he said on his first album is still true today: *"You want a hit? Give me an hour plus a pen and a pad."*

9. Scarface

Southern hip-hop is often criticized for promoting catchy hooks and dances over profound lyrics and concepts, but that criticism could never be leveled at **Scarface**. In reality, Scarface was the first rapper from outside New York or California to receive any type of attention or acclaim. Ever since joining fledgling group The Geto Boys in 1990, Brad Jordan has been making painfully honest and realistically passionate music for more than twenty years, proving that artists south of the Mason-Dixon Line could be both successful and well-respected. While 'Face (and the Geto Boys) was disparaged for overly violent and misogynistic music, his lyrics have always been laced with a trace of sadness. Rather than simply glorifying a gangster persona by claiming to be a drug kingpin or mafia don like many of his contemporaries, Scarface was more honest in his songs, presenting the plight that he and others have faced while expressing the hope that things could be different. Nowhere is this better expressed than in the chilling, paranoia-filled "Mind Playing Tricks on Me" from the Geto Boys' 1991 album, *We Can't Be Stopped*. On the first verse, Scarface takes the listener inside the mind of a person haunted by his conscience and feeling like he's being stalked by death: *"At night I can't sleep, I toss and turn/Candlesticks in the dark, visions of bodies being burned/Four walls just staring at a nigga/I'm paranoid, sleeping with my finger on the trigger/My mother's always stressing I ain't living right/But I ain't going out without a fight/See, every time my eyes close/I start sweating and blood starts coming out my nose/It's somebody watching the Ak'/But I don't know who it is, so I'm watching my back/I can see him when I'm deep in the covers/When I awake, I don't see the motherfucker/He owns a black hat like I own/A black suit and a cane like my own/Some might say, 'Take a chill, b'/But fuck that shit, there's a nigga trying to kill me/I'm popping in the clip when the wind blows/Every twenty seconds got me peeping out my window/Investigating the joint for* *traps/Checking my telephone for taps/I'm staring at the woman on the corner/It's fucked up when your mind's playing tricks on ya.*" His first two solo albums, *Mr. Scarface is Back* and *The World Is Yours,* were both strong efforts, each going gold and including tracks like "A Minute to Pray and a Second to Die," "Let Me Roll," and "Mr. Scarface," but it was his third album, *The Diary*, that propelled him into the higher echelon of emcees. While the Geto Boys were experiencing turmoil and turnover as Scarface began to overshadow the rest of the group, he focused on his solo career, releasing a classic album that is arguably the greatest in the history of southern hip-hop. Featuring "Hand of the Dead Body," and "I Seen a Man Die," *The Diary* sounds like a cry for help disguised as a hardcore rap album. Scarface's next LP, *Untouchable*, was his commercial apex, debuting atop the charts for the only time in his career and employing a much more polished sound. More recently, albums such as *The Last of a Dying Breed*, *The Fix*, and *Emeritus* were all critical successes, proving that he can still connect to both the streets and the masses even after passing his 40th birthday. Perhaps the greatest tribute to Scarface is the fact that so many great artists cite him as an influence and are so eager to work with him, best evidenced on two of his albums, *My Homies* and *My Homies Part 2*, on which nearly every song features a guest appearance. Celebrated artists such as 2Pac, Nas, Jay-Z, Tha Dogg Pound, Ice Cube, Redman, UGK, Beanie Sigel, WC, Master P, Lil' Wayne, T.I., and Dr. Dre have all appeared on at least one Scarface LP, showing how much respect and appreciation they have for his music and his status within the industry. After more than 20 years of recording – 11 solo albums, including three platinum and three gold, as well as 7 albums as part of the Geto Boys, including one platinum and two gold – Scarface has proven himself to be the greatest southern emcee of all time and one of the best ever regardless of geography.

8. Ice Cube

There have been many great emcees to come from California but **Ice Cube** is the greatest of them all. The chief songwriter and performer on N.W.A's classic debut, *Straight Outta Compton*, Cube was the driving force behind the rise of Los Angeles hip-hop as well as partly responsible for the popularity of "gangster rap." Songs like "Fuck the Police," "Gangsta Gangsta" and "Straight Outta Compton" were unlike anything the public had ever heard before. Cube would leave the group shortly thereafter and while many doubted he could make it on his own, it was the group that suffered more than he did. Enlisting the help of Public Enemy's production team The Bomb Squad, the man born as O'Shea Jackson crafted *AmeriKKKa's Most Wanted*, a momentous achievement that sold over a million units and proved that Ice Cube could create a classic without his groupmates with tracks like "Once Upon a Time in the Projects," and "Endangered Species (Tales from the Darkside)," the latter of which saw Cube prophetically explore the police brutality in L.A. two years before the Rodney King verdict and the subsequent riots: *"Peace?!/Don't make me laugh/All I hear is motherfuckers rapping succotash/Living large, telling me to get out the gang/I'm a nigga, gotta live by the trigger/How the fuck do you figure/That I can say 'Peace' and the gunshots will cease?/Every cop killer goes ignored/They just sent another nigga to the morgue/A point scored, they could give a fuck about us/They rather catch us with guns and white powder/If I was old, they'd probably be a friend of me/Since I'm young, they consider me the enemy/They kill ten of me to get the job correct/To serve, protect, and break a nigga's neck/'Cause I'm the one with the trunk of funk/And 'Fuck tha Police' in the tape deck/You should listen to me 'cause there's more to see/Call my neighborhood a ghetto 'cause it houses minorities/The other color don't know, you can run but not hide/These are tales from the darkside."* It was clear that Cube was not afraid to address any topic as he approached every song with an unmatched ferocity. Only a few months later he released *Kill at Will*, a seven-track effort that became the first hip-hop EP to achieve both gold and platinum status and included the highly influential "Jackin' for Beats," where Cube rapped over a variety of famous beats, including one by N.W.A, a concept that has been borrowed by numerous rappers in the years since. A year after *Kill at Will* came the controversial *Death Certificate*, which depicted Cube standing in a morgue next to a body draped in an American flag with a toe tag proclaiming it to be that of

Uncle Sam. The album was another strong effort, including "Steady Mobbin'" and "No Vaseline," a song aimed at N.W.A that is one of the cruelest diss tracks in history. One year after that, Cube officially became a crossover star with *The Predator*. Bolstered by the hits "Wicked," "Check Yo Self," and "It Was a Good Day," it sold over two million copies and is the only one Ice Cube album to reach number one on the *Billboard* 200 chart. In 1993, he released *Lethal Injection*, his fourth album in four years. Thanks largely to the George Clinton-featured hit, "Bop Gun (One Nation)," it was also a commercial success, incorporating more of the "G-Funk" sound that Dr. Dre had popularized and saw Cube changing his style, rhyming less about social and political causes and focusing more on the basic elements of "gangster rap." He was criticized heavily for this transition, but it proved that he could master both sides of the hip-hop spectrum – conscious and successful – equally. In 1996, at the height of the so-called "East Coast-West Coast" conflict, he formed Westside Connection and released a terrifically antagonistic album that proved he still had his ferociousness after nearly a decade of rapping. As his acting career flourished, hip-hop became a secondary concern, but he has continued to drop albums – 1998's *War & Peace Vol. 1 [War]*, 2000's *War & Peace Vol. 2 [Peace]*, 2006's *Laugh Now, Cry Later*, 2008's *Raw Footage*, and 2010's *I Am the West* – that have kept him relevant. While the anger is still there, Cube has mellowed with age. No longer the leader of the rebellion, he is now seen as the wise O.G. that waged wars and lived to tell about them. It's fits him well. After all, few emcees could wage war or tell a story as well as Ice Cube.

7. KRS-One

At its core, hip-hop music is multidimensional. It can be entertaining, funny, enlightening, violent, and educational. Few emcees could combine all of those elements into a career. **KRS-One** did it within songs. A self-professed edutainer (educator and entertainer), Kris Parker could effortlessly segue from vicious battle rap to uplifting and empowering rhymes to humorous punchlines, all within a single verse. At the start of his career, as the leader of Boogie Down Productions, KRS's music contained vivid descriptions and tales of life in the South Bronx. He was also the victor in hip-hop's first major beef, the "Bridge Wars" between himself and the Juice Crew's MC Shan. In response to Shan's "The Bridge," B.D.P.'s first album, *Criminal Minded*, included "The Bridge Is Over" and "South Bronx," two of the fiercest battle songs in hip-hop history. However, that ended on August 27, 1987 when B.D.P.'s DJ, Scott "La Rock" Sterling was shot to death while trying to mediate a neighborhood disagreement. Following La Rock's death, KRS completely changed his style, deciding to focus on more socially- and politically-conscious music and dedicating his music to the memory of his partner. He also founded the Stop the Violence movement, featuring the song, "Self Destruction," that condemned the rampant violence in urban communities. KRS-One released four more albums under the Boogie Down Productions moniker – *By All Means Necessary*, *Ghetto Music: The Blueprint of Hip Hop*, *Edutainment,* and *Sex and Violence* – three of which were certified gold and all credited as "Overseen by Scott La Rock," even though KRS himself had handled, or at least been a part of, much of the production duties. On "Edutainment," KRS perfectly balances the two parts of his persona, giving a virtual history lesson while employing a flow like water and mesmerizing cadence: *Nothing I say now is hypothetical/These are the facts, a little metaphysical/We are one, every heart, every lung/So why then was the black man hung?/He was hung by the so-called Christians/That went to church, and did not listen/See Jesus couldn't stand politics/So they nailed him to a crucifix/Then it was that way, today it's a trigger/So why is the Pope such a political figure?/I don't know, but it's really beyond me/But through knowledge, they'll never con me/'Cause from Jesus Christ to right now/Every time a black man speaks up, ka-plow!/See people concentrate on the leader/And not the message coming through the speaker/If the Christians really heard Christ/The black man never would've lived this life/My point is that, do not concentrate/On what I state, create, or debate/I might be great, and you might admire/But what I say is to take you much higher/More higher than the physical plane/To the plane of forces in the astral plane/The mental plane, and the final three/They're all around you, yet you can't see/So grab the sphere of life and aim it/And you'll be guided by Edutainment*." Feeling it was time to go solo, KRS-One released his first official debut album in 1993, *Return of the Boom Bap*. Featuring stripped-down beats that recalled the early days of hip-hop, and including the controversial "Sound of da Police," it firmly established the "The Blastmaster" as both a lyricist and a teacher. Two years later, he released a critically acclaimed self-titled album that featured future classics "Rappaz R. N. Dainja," and "MC's Act Like They Don't Know," both produced by DJ Premier. In 1997, he pulled off possibly the most impressive feat of his legendary career. Under heavy scrutiny and criticism for being unable to sell records as a solo artist, he made *I Got Next*, a blatant reach for airplay and sales that actually worked. The album, buoyed by the remix to the hit single, "Step into a World (Rapture's Delight)" that featured Puff Daddy, is the only KRS solo album that is certified gold. While the majority of his supporters criticized KRS for the album, he proved that he could make commercially successful music if he actually tried. After *I Got Next*, he would return to his previous form, creating socially conscious songs that did not appeal to as wide of an audience. Since then, KRS-One has become the ambassador of hip-hop, releasing twelve studio albums, writing several books (including *The Gospel of Hip Hop: The First Instrument*), founding the Temple of Hip Hop, and even giving lectures on college campuses, explaining the importance of the culture and dissecting its history. While his most powerful work came two decades ago, the impact of KRS-One continues to this day. One of the most versatile emcees in history, he has an extremely deep catalog, with songs ranging in subject matter from police brutality ("Black Cop"), to drugs ("I Can't Wake Up"), to Jamaican influences ("Remix For P Is Free"), to inner-city killing ("Stop the Violence"), to materialism ("Love's Gonna Get'cha") to basic rap boasting ("I'm Still #1"). If it was an issue, he would rhyme about it and when it came to lyrics, no one had more than KRS-One.

6. Eminem

In 1998, it looked as if Dr. Dre's career was over. When word spread that he was preparing to release the debut album of a white rapper from Detroit, many people believed it was a publicity stunt that smacked of desperation. Most people had never heard of **Eminem**. He had been featured in the coveted "Unsigned Hype" column of *The Source* in March, 1998, but when the general public thought of white emcees, they didn't think of the Beastie Boys or Everlast or even 3rd Bass. Instead, they thought of Vanilla Ice. As a result, Marshall Mathers was dismissed as a novelty act before the public ever heard him. He would ultimately disprove all of them by demonstrating that he could inhabit any style and master any flow. The hit single "My Name Is" catapulted his debut album, *The Slim Shady LP*, to the number two spot on the *Billboard* 200 chart, and the album eventually sold more than four million copies. It was filled with witty wordplay, Em's limitless imagination, and over-the-top violence, all of which was present on "'97 Bonnie & Clyde," which is presented as Em and his daughter, Haillie, taking a ride to the pier so that Haillie's mother – who is *"sleeping in the trunk,"* can go swimming. The song is vivid, hilarious, clever, and appalling, all at the same time. Despite his success, he was dismissed as a one-hit wonder and few believed he could meet expectations or surpass the success of his first disc. He responded in 2000 with *The Marshall Mathers LP*, a dark and brooding effort that found Slim Shady lamenting his newfound fame, taking aim at his critics, and ratcheting up the violence to another level. It also included the hits "The Real Slim Shady," "The Way I Am," and the breathtaking "Stan." It was the fastest-selling hip-hop album in history, selling more than 1.7 million copies in its first week and eventually reaching diamond status (ten million copies sold). He would repeat this feat two years later with *The Eminem Show*. Largely self-produced and featuring some of his most personal rhymes – "White America," "Sing for the Moment," "'Till I Collapse," and "Cleanin' Out My Closet" – it also went platinum in a week and made Eminem the only hip-hop artist to have two certified diamond albums. His next album, *Encore*, was recorded while Em was addicted to prescription drugs and the off-kilter, silly lyrics and immature subject matter certainly show a regression, though there were a few highlights, such as "Like Toy Soldiers," "Mockingbird," "Yellow Brick Road," and the political protest track, "Mosh." Despite disappointing many fans, the album still sold five million albums and, even at his worst, Em was better than nearly everyone else. After a five year hiatus in which he focused on producing, released a compilation album, and buried his best friend (Proof of D12), he released his fifth album on Aftermath. Following the double platinum-selling but slightly disappointing Dr. Dre-produced *Relapse* in 2009, he released *Recovery* a year later. Selling three million copies, it was a more honest and heartfelt effort than its predecessor, incorporating more rock samples and fewer typical hip-hop beats, signaling a new direction for the emcee. Even songs that aren't on his albums have become a part of the culture. His song "Lose Yourself," recorded for the soundtrack to his film *8 Mile*, is the first rap song to ever win an Academy Award and in 2001, he was the only guest star on Jay-Z's landmark album, *The Blueprint*. Featured on the song "Renegade," which he also produced, the two responded to criticisms thrown at them and Eminem spit arguably the best verse in a career that has many highlights: "*Since I'm in a position to talk to these kids and they listen/I ain't no politician, but I'll kick it with 'em a minute/'Cause, see, they call me a menace, and if the shoe fits I'll wear it/But if it don't, then y'all will swallow the truth, grin and bear it/Now who's the king of these rude, ludicrous, lucrative lyrics?/Who could inherit the title, put the youth in hysterics?/Using his music to steer it, sharing his views and his merits/But there's a huge interference – they're saying you shouldn't hear it/Maybe it's hatred I spew, maybe it's food for the spirit/Maybe it's beautiful music I made for you to just cherish/But I'm debated, disputed, hated and viewed in America/As a motherfucking drug addict/Like you didn't experiment?/Now, now, that's when you start to stare at who's in the mirror/And see yourself as a kid again, and you get embarrassed/And I got nothing to do but make you look stupid as parents/You fucking do-gooders, too bad you couldn't do good at marriage/And do you have any clue what I had to do to get here?/I don't think you do, so stay tuned and keep your ears glued to the stereo...*" The highest-selling music artist of the 2000s with more 32.2 million copies sold, he is the most successful rapper ever, with more than 86 million albums sold worldwide. He has reached the number one spot on the *Billboard* 200 chart ten times –

seven times as a solo artist (including two compilations), two as part of D12 and one as one-half of the duo Bad Meets Evil. However, his commercial success is only part of the story. Eminem is more than just a good-looking white guy that sold a lot records to young girls. Arguably the most feared battle rapper on the planet, he has ended careers with his music. He has it all: lyrics, delivery, flow, cadence, subject matter, fearlessness, metaphors, and internal rhyme schemes. He may have been seen as a gimmick when he first started, but it's clear to everyone now: Eminem is the definition of a complete emcee.

5. Nas

Being hailed as a savior before the age of 21 could be too much of a burden for many artists to handle. Fortunately, **Nas** is not most artists. Proclaimed "the next Rakim" before ever releasing an album, he exceeded all expectations with arguably the greatest debut album in hip-hop history. A virtually flawless LP in every area, *Illmatic* introduced Nasir Jones as an honest, yet optimistic and introspective observer of urban life ("The World Is Yours," "Life's a Bitch") as well as a gifted storyteller ("N.Y. State of Mind") that could create vivid scenes through his lyrics and concepts ("One Love") while still maintaining the competitive boasting on which hip-hop was originally founded ("It Ain't Hard to Tell"). Though an undeniable classic, *Illmatic* was a disappointment in terms of sales – it achieved platinum status only after Nas enjoyed future success – and was overshadowed commercially by The Notorious B.I.G.'s *Ready to Die*. Consequently, Nas began to focus on making more crossover-friendly music, a decision that would dramatically alter the rest of his career. His sophomore album, 2006's *It Was Written*, was a vastly different album from *Illmatic*, as he took on the moniker of "Nas Escobar" and delivered an album full of Mafioso themes and over-the-top story rhymes over polished beats. Though seen as a betrayal by his original fans, *It Was Written* was an enormous success thanks mainly to the wildly successful single "If I Ruled the World (Imagine That)," remaining in the top spot of the *Billboard* 200 for four weeks and selling over two million copies. From that point on, Nas would do his best to satisfy his two competing fan bases, trying to make songs that appealed to fans of the grittiness of *Illmatic* and the melodic crispness of *It Was Written*. Two years after the colossal flop of his supergroup The Firm, he released *I Am…*, an obvious attempt to merge the styles of the first two LPs with "N.Y. State of Mind Pt. II," "Hate Me Now," and "Nas Is Like," and *Nastradamus*, within six months of one another. The latter, which included "You Owe Me" and the title track, both of which were blatant reaches for radio airplay, was viewed as Nas's weakest album. Many believed that his career was over, a feeling that was reinforced by Jay-Z when he made their long-lasting hostile rivalry public on "Takeover." Ironically, Jay's apparent knockout punch actually had the opposite effect, lighting a fire under Nas and provoking the public to greatly anticipate his response. That response was 2001's *Stillmatic* and, as the title implies, it was (mostly) a return to form and Nas's strongest outing since *It Was Written*. In addition to "Ether," the merciless answer to "Takeover" that actually saw Nas win the battle of the two superstars, the album also included the *Sopranos*-inspired "Got Urself A…," and "One Mic," where Nas is wishing for nothing more than a simple life: *"All I need is one life, one try, one breath, I'm one man/What I stand for speaks for itself, they don't understand/Or wanna see me on top, too egotistical/Talking all that slick shit, the same way these bitches do/Wonder what my secrets is, niggas will move on you/Only if they know what your weakness is/I have none/Too late to grab guns I'm blasting 'cause I'm a cool nigga/Thought I wouldn't have that ass done? Fooled you niggas/What you call an infinite brawl, eternal souls clashing/War gets deep, some beef is everlasting/Complete with thick scars, brothers knifing each other up in prison yards/Drama, where does it start?/You know the block was ill as a youngster/Every night it was like a cop would get killed, body found in the dumpster/For real a hustler, purchased my Range/Niggas throwing dirt on my name/Jealous 'cause fiends got their work and complain/Bitches left me 'cause they thought I was finished/Should've knew she wasn't true/She came to me when her man caught a sentence/Diamonds are blinding, I never make the same mistakes/Moving with a change of pace/Lighter load, see, now the king is straight/Swelling my melon cause none of these niggas real/Heard they* were telling police – how can a kingpin squeal?/This is crazy, I'm on the right track I'm finally found/You need some soul-searching, the time is now/[Chorus] All I need is one mic." It was recorded only five years after "If I Ruled the World (Imagine That)," but "One Mic" demonstrated Nas's mind state at the time compared to where it had been in 1996. In the past decade since his renaissance with *Stillmatic*, he has continued to push boundaries, releasing his most heartfelt and honest work (*God's Son*), a double album (*Street's Disciple*), two very controversially-named albums (*Hip Hop Is Dead* and an untitled album that was originally called *Nigger*), and a collaborative effort with Damien Marley (*Distant Relatives*) that focused solely on the plight of Africa. Though he will probably never replicate *Illmatic*, he has proven to have ability to expound on any subject or emotion – success, failure, marriage, divorce, the death of loved ones, expectations, helplessness, rage, happiness, and more – better than anyone aside from arguably 2Pac. He has been a great storyteller and poet for nearly 20 years, vacillating between novel-esque crime stories ("Shootouts," "Undying Love," "Rewind") and realistic explorations of inner-city life that feel more like documentaries ("Black Girl Lost," "2nd Childhood") than fictional songs. More than just the next Rakim, he was a combination of Rakim, Kool G. Rap, and Slick Rick all rolled into one. He's had his share of missteps and it could be argued that he never fulfilled the potential he showed as a 20 year-old, but Nas is obviously one of the all-time greats whose music will only become more appreciated in the years to come.

4. The Notorious B.I.G.

He only released two albums before his untimely death at the age of 24, but **The Notorious B.I.G.**'s talent and influence were undeniable. A towering figure in hip-hop from the first time he appeared on record, he was proclaimed to be the East Coast's answer to the dominance of Death Row Records in the early '90s. The star of Puff Daddy's new label, Bad Boy Records, Christopher Wallace was one of the most anticipated artists in hip-hop history, having already proven himself on various recordings, most notably stealing the show from heavyweights LL Cool J and Busta Rhymes on the remix to Craig Mack's hit "Flava In Ya Ear," before ever releasing an album. His debut, *Ready to Die*, was released in September, 1994, and The Notorious B.I.G. became an instant star. The album, which would ultimately sell four million copies, was presented as an audio storytelling of his life and B.I.G. managed to balance grimy street music ("Gimme the Loot," "Ready to Die," "Everyday Struggle") with radio-friendly crossover hits ("Juicy," "Big Poppa") without losing any of his credibility. He was crowned the "King of New York" and was immediately considered one of the greats. Following the breakout success of "One More Chance/Stay with Me," the remix to a song that appeared on the album that reached number two on the *Billboard* Hot 100 singles chart, B.I.G. became an unlikely sex symbol while also retaining his more hardcore fans. Arguably the greatest storytelling emcee in history, he was extremely descriptive of violent situations that he peppered with humor, as well as numerous double entendres and metaphors. He was known for his slow and relaxed flow in a powerful, cocksure voice and mesmerizing cadence that made his rhymes sound effortless but still important. After working on, and contributing to, *Conspiracy*, the debut by his protégés, Junior M.A.F.I.A., he became the target of former friend 2Pac, who felt that B.I.G. had been a part of a plot to have him robbed and shot since Junior M.A.F.I.A. had been recording in the building where the incident occurred. The result was the "East Coast-West Coast" clash that would dominate the genre for nearly two years and would ultimately be blamed for the deaths of both men. The Notorious B.I.G. was shot and killed on March 9, 1997, in Los Angeles, just two weeks before the release of his sophomore LP, the double album *Life AfterDeath*. An immediate classic that was presented as a sequel to its predecessor, it would eventually be certified diamond (with each sale was counted twice). It showcased a mature-sounding Biggie adopting a more polished style that was the precursor to future Bad Boy albums as well as partaking in the Mafioso-style that was popular at the time. Just as he had on *Ready to Die*, the "Black Frank White" walked the fine line between music for the streets ("What's Beef?," "Niggas Bleed," "Ten Crack Commandments," "My Downfall") and music for the radio ("Hypnotize," "Mo Money, Mo

Problems," "Sky's the Limit"). His ability to change his style depending on the situation was more evident than ever, as he matched Too $hort's penchant for arrogant pimp talk on "The World Is Filled..." and rhymed faster than ever on "Notorious Thugs" to keep up with tongue-twisters Bone Thugs-N-Harmony while still making every word count long before artists experimented with different flows on their albums: "*Armed and dangerous/Ain't too many can bang with us/Straight up weed, no angel dust/Label us/'Notorious'/Thug ass niggas that love to bust/It's strange to us/Y'all niggas be scrambling/gambling/Up in restaurants with mandolins/And violins/We just sitting here trying to win/Trying not to sin/High off weed and lots of gin/So much smoke need oxygen/Steadily counting them Benjamins/Nigga you should too/If you knew/What this game gon' do to you/Been in this shit since '92/Look at all the bullshit I been through/So-called 'beef' with You-Know-Who/Fucked a few female stars or two/Nigga, blue light/Nigga move like Mike/Shit/Not to be fucked with/Motherfucker better duck quick/ 'Cause me and my dogs love to buck shit/Fuck the luck shit/Strictly aim/No aspirations to quit the game/Spit your game, talk your shit/Grab your gat, call your clique/Squeeze your clip, hit the right one/Pass that weed, I got to light one/All them niggas, I got to fight one/All them hoes, I got to like one/Our situation is a tight one/What you gonna do: fight or run?/Seems to me that you'll take B/Bone and Big, nigga, die slowly/I'ma tell you like a nigga told me/'Cash Rules Everything Around Me'/Shit/Lyrically, niggas can't see me/Fuck it, buy the coke/Cook the coke, cut it/Know the bitch 'fore you caught yourself loving it/Nigga with a Benz fucking it/Doesn't it seem odd to you?/Big come through with mobs and crews/Goodfellas down to the Mo' Thugs dudes/Who's the killer, me or you?*" More than fifteen years after his death, B.I.G.'s shadow continues to loom large over hip-hop: Bad Boy has released three posthumous albums (*Born Again*, *Duets: The Final Chapter*, and *Greatest Hits*), a film was made on his life, Jay-Z and Nas engaged in a battle for his vacated throne, and artists from all over the country constantly try to match his versatility, most of whom fail. His body of work is relatively small, but it is nearly flawless, and it will remain that way forever.

3. 2Pac

The most prolific, contradictory, and controversial artist in hip-hop history was also one of the most successful musical artists in American history. **2Pac** has sold more than 75 million albums worldwide, an amazing feat considering that he only lived to the age of 25 years old and had only completed five albums at the time of his death. He was a soldier, a leader, a prophet, a poet, and a thug. He began his career as a backup dancer for the fun-loving group Digital Underground and died as the most scandalous rapper in history. Tupac Shakur was the son of Black Panthers and that background heavily influenced the early part of his career. His 1991 debut, *2Pacalypse Now*, was raw and uncompromising, focusing heavily on social issues and political injustices, including teenage pregnancy ("Brenda's Got a Baby") and police brutality ("Trapped"). While the album was a strong debut that reached gold status and garnered enough attention to be condemned by Vice President Dan Quayle, it was far from polished as Shakur struggled to find both his voice and his style for an entire LP. His charisma, however, was undeniable. Two years later came 2Pac's breakout album, *Strictly 4 My N.I.G.G.A.Z.*, a more successful project that offset his sociopolitical material ("Souljah's Revenge," "The Streetz R Deathrow," "Holler If Ya Hear Me") with popular commercial cuts ("Keep Ya Head Up," "I Get Around"), all of which illustrated the contradictions within Shakur that would only become more pronounced in the future. In November, 1994, he was shot five times during a robbery, but he survived and, fearing for his life, checked himself out of the hospital after only three hours. The following day, he appeared in court in a wheelchair and covered in bandages to hear that he had been found guilty of three counts of molestation. A year later, while he was imprisoned, his third album, *Me Against the World*, debuted atop the *Billboard* 200 chart, making 2Pac the first artist in history to have a number one album while in prison. A result of legal troubles, pending incarceration, and financial woes, it is 'Pac's most personal and honest work, one that expresses his paranoia ("Death Around the Corner," "If I

Die 2Nite"), nostalgia ("Dear Mama," "Old School"), and infidelity ("Temptations"). On "So Many Tears," 2Pac opens his heart and lays bare his soul for all to see and hear: *"Now I'm lost and I'm weary, so many tears/I'm suicidal, so don't stand near me/My every move is a calculated step/To bring me closer to embrace an early death/Now there's nothing left/There was no mercy on the streets, I couldn't rest/I'm barely standing, 'bout to go to pieces, screaming 'Peace!'/And though my soul was deleted, I couldn't see it/I had my mind full of demons trying to break free/They planted seeds and they hatched, sparking the flame/Inside my brain like a match, such a dirty game/No memories, just a misery/Painting a picture of my enemies killing me in my sleep/Will I survive 'til the morning, to see the Sun/Please, Lord forgive me for my sins, 'cause here I come/[Chorus] Lord, I suffered through the years and shed so many tears/God, I lost so many peers and shed so many tears."* However, Shakur's introspective and apologetic demeanor would not last long. After serving 11 months of his sentence, Death Row CEO Suge Knight paid $1.4 million to bail 2Pac out of jail. In exchange, 'Pac agreed to a contract stipulating that he would release three albums for Death Row. His behavior changed immediately. Four months after leaving jail, he released *All Eyez on Me*, a slickly produced, sprawling double album that went light on the consciousness of his earlier work in favor of over-the-top "gangster rap" that was Death Row's trademark. Hugely successful, it would eventually sell nine million copies and establish 2Pac as the biggest star in the genre. It was also at this point that he fearlessly decided to diss an entire coast, claiming that The Notorious B.I.G. had been involved in his shooting and extending a challenge to virtually all New York artists. The resulting "East Coast-West Coast" hostility would dominate the industry for over a year and would change hip-hop forever. Very few emcees would have attacked an entire coast and almost none of them could have had the impact that 'Pac had. He was relentless, basically making fans choose sides that are still debated to this day. His fifth album, *The Don Killuminati: The 7 Day Theory*, released under Shakur's alias of "Makaveli," dropped two months after his death. The songs were written and recorded in three days and 'Pac sounds like a man that knows his days are numbered, fearing that music will suffer from what he believes to be his impending death. The LP is vicious ("Bomb First," "Against All Odds"), thought-provoking ("White Man'z World"), creative ("Me and My Girlfriend"), and brilliant. It was also successful, reaching quadruple-platinum status. It is the final word from one of the generation's greatest voices and his prophecies regarding his own murder are chilling, even fifteen years later. 2Pac left a vault full of music behind and, as result, numerous posthumous discs have been released under his name, but there are only five that truly reflect his artistic vision. The hardest-working hip-hop artist to ever touch a microphone, he recorded more songs in a year than many do in a career. As such, he wasn't perfect – he had nearly as many misses as hits – but he is the only hip-hop artist with a song to match every mood and emotion. His music spoke to people of all races, genders, ethnicities, and backgrounds. In an attempt to do the same, every rapper that came after him, including the future greats, studied him and tried to emulate his style, making 2Pac the most influential emcee in history.

2. Rakim

There are a handful of artists that singlehandedly changed industry simply through their talent and innovation. Everything changed after their arrival and everything before it immediately seemed outdated with a clear delineation between the two. For Rock and Roll, that artist was Elvis Presley and for hip-hop, that artist was **Rakim**. Up until 1986, every rapper used the same basic style – yelling lyrics full of monosyllabic words within a rudimentary song structure while relying on the music to do the bulk of the work. Rakim changed everything. After all, there is a reason they call him the "God MC." Employing a relaxed flow in a mesmerizing voice with wordplay that made fans repeatedly press rewind and lyrics that made them reach for their dictionaries, Ra introduced the modern technique of rhyming, not only paving the way for Kool G. Rap, Big Daddy Kane, and KRS-One, but also for Nas, Jay-Z, Raekwon, and The Notorious B.I.G. Along with his DJ Eric B, Rakim cemented his greatness on the first track, "I Ain't No Joke" of the duo's first album, *Paid in Full*: "*I ain't no joke, I used to let the mic smoke/Now I slam it when I'm done and make* *sure it's broke/When I'm gone no one gets on 'cause I won't let/Nobody press up and mess up the scene I set/I like to stand in a crowd and watch the people wonder 'Damn'/But think about it, then you'll understand/I'm just an addict addicted to music/Maybe it's a habit, I gotta use it/Even if it's jazz or the quiet storm/I hook a beat up convert it in a hip-hop form/Write a rhyme in graffiti in every show you see me in/Deep concentration 'cause I'm no comedian/Jokers are wild if you wanna be tame/I'll treat you like a child then you're gonna be named/Another enemy, not even a friend of me/'Cause you'll get fried in the end if you pretend to be/Competing/'Cause I just put your mind on pause/And I can beat you when you compare my rhyme with yours/I wake you up and as I stare in your face you seem stunned/Remember me, the one you got your idea from?/But soon you start to suffer, the tune will get rougher/When you start to stutter that's when you had enough of/Biting it will make you choke, you can't provoke/You can't cope, you should have broke/'Cause I ain't no joke."* Also boasting influential songs like "Eric B. Is President," "I Know You Got Soul," and "My Melody," *Paid in Full* was the start of the golden age of hip-hop and Rakim was the king. A year later, he somehow improved his skills on *Follow the Leader*, using his voice as another instrument in concert with the beat and showing more hostility towards those that didn't take their craft as seriously as he did on several tracks including, "Microphone Fiend," "Lyrics of Fury," and the title track. While both LPs were classics, they were both uneven efforts that failed to maintain their consistency throughout, particularly musically. Their third album, 1990's *Let the Rhythm Hit 'Em*, was terrific from start to finish and showcased Rakim was at his best, whether attacking the microphone (the title track) or relating a chance encounter with a young lady ("Mahogany"). It was the high point for both Eric B. and Rakim, not to mention hip-hop as a whole, as it was about to change dramatically at the start of the '90s. In 1992, the duo released their final album, *Don't Sweat the Technique*, and while Rakim was still ferocious on the microphone – his voice had changed to a much deeper baritone, he was now competing against the same emcees that he had helped to create. His revolutionary style was no longer the exception, it was now the norm. Perhaps sensing this, the duo parted ways and Ra took a five year hiatus. He returned in

1997 with *The 18th Letter*, his solo debut that was a solid effort containing "Guess Who's Back," "It's Been a Long Time," and "New York (Ya Out There)." Two more albums would follow, 1999's *The Master* and 2009's *The Seventh Seal*, and while Rakim was no longer the industry's trendsetter, he was an elder statesman that proved he could still control the microphone. His legacy is everywhere in hip-hop, from internal rhyme schemes, to dexterous wordplay, to descriptive metaphors, to his lyrics that are so often sampled and quoted. Every popular emcee of the past twenty-five years has been influenced by The R, either directly or indirectly. He made the entire culture treat hip-hop as an art form rather than a fun hobby and made some of the greatest music in history while doing it. After all, he took it *"more serious than just a poem."*

1. Jay-Z

For someone that was rejected by every major record label and was forced to start his own as a last resort, **Jay-Z** certainly proved everyone wrong. Though no one realized it at the time, Shawn Carter would become the most complete emcee to ever bless a microphone. Complex rhyme structures? Check. Ability to master any flow? Check. Willing and able to create properly structured songs and complete conceptualized albums? Check. Ability to crossover without alienating the hardcore fans? Check. Maintaining relevancy for more than a decade and constantly setting trends? Check. He has it all. Jay-Z is as close to a perfect rapper as there has ever been in hip-hop. That was not always the case. In the early '90s his style was of the rapid-fire, tongue-twisting variety, much like an imitation of Das EFX, and while he made several attention-grabbing guest appearances with the likes of Big Daddy Kane and Big L, he was still not garnering the attention of the industry. After the success of *Illmatic* and *Ready to Die*, Jay slowed down his flow in an effort to connect with listeners and make sure that every single word received the attention it deserved. It worked. *Reasonable Doubt*, his debut album, arrived in the summer of 1996 and was filled with honest depictions of crime life in America. An instant classic that sounds even better with age, songs like

"Can't Knock the Hustle," "D'Evils," and "Politics as Usual" brought a lyrical depth that had not previously been explored in hip-hop. "Can I Live," an examination of the conflicting emotions that plague a drug dealer that supplies his neighbors with product, still stands as one of the greatest songs of his unparalleled career: *"While I'm watching every nigga watching me closely/My shit is butter, for the bread they wanna toast me/I keep my head - both of them where they supposed to be/Hoes will get you sidetracked, then clap from close feet/I don't sleep, I'm tired/I feel wired like codeine/These days, a brother gotta admire me from four fiends away/My pain, wish it was quick to see/From selling 'caine 'til brains was fried to a fricassee/Can't lie/At the time it never bothered me/At the bar, getting my thug on properly/My squad and me, lack of respect for authority/Laughing hard, happy to be escaping poverty/However brief, I know this game got valleys and peaks/Expectation for dips/For precipitation we stack chips, hardly/The youth I used to be, soon to see a million/No more Big Willie, my game has grown, prefer you call me 'William'/Illin' for revenues, Rayful Edmond-like, Channel 7 News/'Round seven Jews, head dead in the mic/Forgetting all I ever knew, convenient amnesia/"I suggest you call my lawyer, I know the procedure"/Lock my body, can't trap my mind/Easily explain why we adapt to crime/I'd rather die enormous than live dormant, that's how we on it/Live at the main event, I bet a trip to Maui on it/Presidential suites my residential for the weekend/Confidentially speaking in codes since I sense you peeking/The NSX rental, don't be fooled, my game is mental/We both out of town, dog, what you trying to get into?/Viva Las Vegas, see ya later/At the crap tables, meet me by the one that starts a 'G' up/This way no fraud Willies present gambling they re-up/And we can have a pleasant time, sipping margaritas/Yeah, yeah, yeah!/Can I live? Can I live?"* Initially, *Reasonable Doubt* only reached gold status and other artists (most notably Nas) garnered much more attention in the summer of '96. A year later, following the deaths of 2Pac and his friend The Notorious B.I.G., Jay-Z attempted to bridge the two worlds of street music and radio hits on *In My Lifetime, vol. 1*. The LP featured classic street anthems and went platinum, but was beset by failed attempts at crossover hits that sounded forced. Finally, in 1998, he mastered the balance between the two realms, releasing the very successful *Vol. 2…Hard Knock Life* with hits such as the title track and "Money Ain't a Thang." With sales of over five million copies, it made Jay-Z an instant superstar and placed him at the top of the hip-hop world, a spot he would occupy for much of the next decade. Two triple platinum (*Vol. 3…Life and Times of S. Carter*, *The Black Album*) and three double platinum (*The Dynasty: Roc La Familia*, *The Blueprint*, *The Blueprint 2: The Gift & The Curse*) albums would follow, with Jay constantly reinventing himself through his music, using different producers, flows, concepts, and subject matter. After a short-lived retirement, he returned in 2006 with the mature-sounding *Kingdom Come* that was successful, but ultimately seen as a disappointment and had many wondering if he had lost his touch. The following year came the return to form with the concept disc, *American Gangster*, and two years after that, *The Blueprint 3*, which featured his first number one hit song as a solo artist, "Empire State of Mind." While his work with other artists – *Best of Both Worlds* with R. Kelly, *Collision Course* with Linkin Park, *Watch the Throne* with Kanye West – is impressive and his success – eleven number one albums on the *Billboard* 200 chart, the most ever by a solo artist and second only to The Beatles – is astonishing for a hip-hop artist, his skill and innovation are what truly set him apart. Even on songs that few hear, such as "This Life Forever," a song for the soundtrack to a *book* (*The Black Gangster*), he shines, effortlessly weaving metaphors that connect mathematics, drug selling, gun violence, and chess. Many of his biggest hits are layered with multiple meanings and complex structures that are missed upon first listen, but ultimately reveal themselves to be more than just catchy songs that garner airplay. Hip-hop is a young man's profession, with very few emcees over the age 30 being able to connect to the audience or remain successful. Now into his 40's, Jay-Z has done that for fifteen years and while he and his peers wanted to be Rakim when they were younger, every up-and-coming artist of any genre now wants to be Jay-Z. He took the blueprint designed by the greats of the '80s, expanded upon it, and perfected it, creating the most impressive catalog of music in hip-hop history.

Honorable Mentions

Big Daddy Kane

Kool G. Rap

Ghostface Killah

Chuck D

Redman

Outro

Any endeavor such as this one is bound to create disagreements and lead to arguments. For me, these disagreements and arguments took place internally. Looking at my original outline of this project, it's incredible to see how much my rankings changed over the course of writing this book. Even while in the process of writing or proofreading some of the chapters, I would veer off course and begin cutting and pasting, changing the order and occasionally removing one entry in favor of another that had been previously discarded. I'm sure these lists will be vastly different in another ten or twenty years and that's the beauty of the music – it keeps evolving.

While performing the necessary research for this book, I listened to thousands of songs, revisited albums I haven't heard in years, and even discovered some interesting new things that I had not known previously about artists and their careers. It served as a wonderful trip down memory lane and it was fascinating to see where the music and the culture originated and how it evolved along with the rest of the nation. The United States of America is a different place in 2012 than it was in 2002 or 1992 or 1982 and, similarly, hip-hop is different now than it was during those times too.

It's become an indelible part of the fabric of America, so much so that politicians are now questioned about it as if it were another part of the social agenda. U.S. Senator and former Democratic nominee for President John Kerry once said, *"I'm fascinated by rap and by hip-hop. I think there's a lot of poetry in it. There's a lot of anger, a lot of social energy in it. And I think you'd better listen to it pretty carefully, because it's important."* When considering the genre's background and how it was initially dismissed as a fad, such a quote by one of the more powerful men in government is nothing short of stunning. Moreover, President Barack Obama has been proud to admit that he has Jay-Z and Ludacris in his iPod. It's amazing how far the movement has come in such a short period of time. It's obvious that hip-hop is here to stay and even those that may not like that fact are being forced to face the truth that people of every age, race, color, creed, region, and socioeconomic background listen to the music and connect with it on an emotional level.

Snoop Dogg said it best: *"Well, hip-hop is what makes the world go around."*

THE HIP-HOP 10

ABOUT THE AUTHOR

Christopher Pierznik works in finance and is a feature contributor to IHateJJRedick.com. A graduate of La Salle University and Temple University's Fox School of Business, this is his first book. He lives with his wife and newborn child in Philadelphia, Pennsylvania. His dream is to one day be a member of the Wu-Tang Clan.

Printed in Great Britain
by Amazon.co.uk, Ltd.,
Marston Gate.